THE NEXT
BIG THING
IN SCHOOL
IMPROVEMENT

REBECCA ALLEN | MATTHEW EVANS | BEN WHITE

First published 2021

by John Catt Educational Ltd,
15 Riduna Park, Station Road,
Melton, Woodbridge IP12 1QT

Tel: +44 (0) 1394 389850
Fax: +44 (0) 1394 386893
Email: enquiries@johncatt.com
Website: www.johncatt.com

ISBN: 978 1 913622 87 9

Set and designed by John Catt Educational Limited

ABOUT THE AUTHORS

Rebecca Allen is chief analyst at and co-founder of Teacher Tapp, the largest teacher survey in the UK. She is also a professor of education at the University of Brighton and over her academic career she has written extensively on school accountability, admissions, assessment, expenditure and teacher careers. In 2018, she chaired a government working group to review how data is used in schools. Her book with Sam Sims on teacher careers called *The Teacher Gap* was published in 2018.

Matthew Evans is headteacher of Farmor's School, a secondary comprehensive in Gloucestershire. His subject background is business and economics, which he has taught since 1995. Matthew is a published author: his book called *Leaders with Substance: An Antidote to Leadership Genericism in Schools* was published in 2019, and he also contributed a chapter to the recent *The researchED Guide to Leadership*.

Ben White is an assistant head at Maidstone Grammar School for Girls in Kent. He combines classroom teaching with a national role in education through various partnerships and collaborations. He has written research guides for Ambition Institute and led research projects for the Education Endowment Foundation (EEF), Ashford Teaching Alliance (ATA) and the Department for Education (DfE). He currently facilitates the National Professional Qualification (NPQ) in Leading Teacher Development and also co-designed Compare and Learn (a comparative learning web app).

This book is dedicated to teachers,
of whom we ask the impossible.

CONTENTS

INTRODUCTION

Plus ça change, plus c'est la même chose.
The more things change, the more they stay the same.

Jean-Baptiste Alphonse Karr[1]

Colgate branded ready meals...Clairol's Touch of Yoghurt Shampoo... Fortune Snookies (fortune cookies for dogs)...Gillette For Oily Hair Only Shampoo...Toaster Eggs...[2]

Have you heard of any of these products? Probably not. You are even less likely to have bought them because they have long since been taken off the market. One might wonder how anyone ever thought they were a good idea.

These products have something else in common: they are each archived in a museum located in Ann Arbor, Michigan, US.

In the 1960s, marketing executive Robert McMath started collecting new products to create his own 'reference library' of successful corporate innovation. However, as products accumulated, the repository quickly became a vast collection of unsuccessful products. The fact is that most products fail, rather than succeed. It is naturally hard for humans to appreciate this since our instincts are always to turn away from our mistakes. Today, Robert McMath's The Museum of Failed Products is visited by product designers from across America, thus forcing their profession to confront the mistakes of the past.[3] How often are we in education able to do the same?

As in the world of consumer goods, the history of modern schooling is marked by a succession of 'Next Big Things'. While we cannot predict what they will be, or how long they will last, we all learn to expect the Next Big Thing to emerge and dominate for a spell, before eventually being replaced, just as each of its predecessors was. Your vintage as a teacher, and the specific schools you have worked in, will dictate which Next Big Things you have direct experience of, and that you may have embraced, ignored or subverted.

Do you remember being told that the curriculum is the progression model? If you trained recently, this is likely your first experience of a Big Thing. If you have worked in our school system for a little longer, there will have been others. How about being told that all pupils must make progress within each lesson? Now, it would seem, they do not. Cast your mind back further. Do you remember the flight path pupils were (allegedly) on, being told that your lesson was 'good with outstanding features', being urged to make your marking dialogic (with triple impact!), to direct questions using lollipop sticks or to switch between thinking hats? Perhaps you were the one asking these things of teachers. Perhaps you still are.

No warehouse exists for storing the succession of Big Things that punctuate the timeline of modern universal schooling. We could create one by curating the slogans, artefacts and policies associated with Big Things past. The perfect antidote to time spent dreaming about how well things *might* go, the museum would provide a story of extinction, dissipation and U-turn. We might playfully call it 'The Last Failed Thing' – a powerful reminder of the shelf-life of good ideas when they are exposed to the complex reality of the school system (of which more later).

For those who find the thought of such 'negative visualisation' unpalatable, we would ask whether it is better to countenance a history of failure, or consign ourselves to a future full of it? For without this resource our memory is selective; we leap from one Big Thing to another, failing to learn the lessons that our imaginary museum would make it harder to ignore. The complexity of our system would be readily apparent in the disparity between the predicted, imagined and actual impact of successive 'promising ideas'.

We might also include historical voices in our exhibits. The accounts of teachers', students', policymakers' and school leaders' experiences of dominant Big Things over time would reveal the diverse ways they make sense of the complex system they operate in. We would capture the voices of those enthusiastically embracing the latest Big Thing, of those paying lip-service to it and of others directly pushing back or even feigning ignorance that the Last Big Thing has been dethroned.

Glimpsing forwards 10 years or so, we cannot confidently predict how individual schools will fare but can promise that there will be a new Big Thing and a similar distribution of responses to it. That Next Big Thing will have a limited shelf-life, too. *Plus ça change...*

This reality of Next Big Thing after Next Big Thing is one that the three of us writing this book together have regularly encountered and learned, to a degree, to live with. We have watched with increasing scepticism as leaders, companies and consultants confidently assert that they have worked out how to improve schools. So far, none of them have found a reliable formula for how to make schools better. The methodology of whole-school improvement companies such as Achievement for All (AfA), Challenge the Gap (CtG) and the Teacher Effectiveness Enhancement Programme (TEEP) has failed to stand up to the close scrutiny of participation in randomised controlled trials.[4] Analysis of the impact of dozens of turnaround policies in US schools is mixed.[5] Multi-academy trusts with high average performance table position all have individual schools that they are struggling to turnaround.[6] Schools that fail their Ofsted inspection are given support to improve, yet many do not manage to resolve the difficulties they are experiencing.[7] We all know of schools that have struggled for long periods of time, seemingly impervious to concerted efforts to 'improve' them. Nobody has yet demonstrated they have the universal blueprint for school improvement. We suspect that this is because there isn't one.

We could feel jaded and try to ignore the optimism of those who feel their policy initiative will be the transformative one. But, instead, we have tried to carry out a systematic analysis of this dynamic of policy fads that has permeated our working lives as educators. It shaped the system before we entered it and will continue to do the same after we move on. We have not built a museum; instead, we have written this book. It does not document every Big Thing, but it does seek to understand why they come to be.

What is our story?

This book tells a story about why school improvement is so difficult and why policies intended to realise it over-promise and under-deliver. The three of us writing this book together each have a different lens, a different starting point and different tools to bring to bear on the question of education. We are painfully aware of our fallibilities regarding viewing education from our own, narrow, perspective – Ben as teacher, Matthew as headteacher and Becky as policy analyst. And, of course, we all share the natural human desire to believe we have something worthwhile to offer. In coming together, we hope to mitigate our individual failings at least a little. As the late American sociologist Seymour B. Sarason observed, how we view a school is determined by our relation to it, and the complexity of schooling is more than one person alone can grasp. However, we like to think that there is strength in our difference of perspective and that in unifying these the school system might make a little more sense.[8]

The story we tell in this book characterises the education system not as a machine amenable to being fixed, nor a problem that can be resolved, but as a beast that resists our attempts to tame it. Throughout the book, we draw on a variety of theoretical perspectives, particularly complexity theory and sense-making. Complexity theory affords us with some insight into behavioural shifts and structural changes as emergent properties of the education system. These emergent properties are shaped, in part, by sense-making of individual actors who are trying to come to terms with the work they do. Sense-making is the psychological process whereby individuals interpret experience in relation to their prior frames of reference.[9] By analysing sense-making in relation to complexity, we seek to explain how the necessary simplification of complex phenomena can produce naïve and harmful actions, along with the beguiling allure of the Next Big Thing.

The book begins by highlighting how relatively little we know about the diverse and complex task of schooling children.

In chapter 1, we seek to persuade the reader that our ignorance and uncertainty about how schools work is substantial, often goes unacknowledged and is somewhat inevitable given the complexity of the education system. It is this complexity that means we rely on regularities, habits, narratives and stories to go about our daily lives in schools.

Chapter 2 explores *why* we know so little about how the system works, despite more than a century of intensive activity by educational researchers. We discuss why the latest version of the 'what works' movement has so far fallen short of what it promised to deliver. We suggest a more limited and specific approach to educational research and greater caution in replicating supposedly good ideas in a new context.

In chapter 3, we explore the diversity of the classroom and how this creates an impossible challenge for teachers. Pupils learn different and often unknown amounts, at different speeds, from varied and opaque starting points. In attempting to understand the classroom dynamic, educators draw on various disciplines, from neuroscience through to sociology, each of which leads to a different narrative with its own internally plausible solutions to ensure success in the classroom. However, none of these solutions will overcome the irresolvable dilemmas created by attempts to educate children at scale.

Next, our book turns to some of the major policy reforms that the three of us have experienced in our careers and how these reveal some fundamental problems of schooling.

In chapter 4, we recall the fate of Personalised Learning as a policy initiative and trace its origin to the foundation of mass education. This story reveals a fundamental problem in schooling, which we term the 'lock-step' problem. This problem re-emerges throughout the history of schooling and each time there is a new attempt to provide a solution. Each solution relies on a particular conception of the problem, and each bears the hallmarks of the previous (failed) attempt to overcome this fundamental problem.

Chapter 5 highlights a second fundamental problem of schooling: the invisibility of learning. This limits our ability to decide what to teach, to check if children are progressing, to identify good and bad practice and to hold schools to account. In the early 2000s, a new solution emerged that promised to solve the invisibility problem: data. Data was a movement the school system would later come to regret, and many of those who made the biggest spreadsheets wondered, in retrospect, why they ever thought it was a good idea.

The latest policy wave to sweep over the education system, The Curriculum, is described in chapter 6. The curriculum is the antidote to differentiated learning outcomes and progression models that promote variations in individual achievement. While there is considerable merit in carefully constructing curricula, we argue that once an idea is proposed as the solution to almost everything, it will inevitably fail. However, if we understand the formation, structure and inevitable fate of these policy waves, we can hope to become better at riding them.

The next three chapters turn to considering the nature of the institutions that we ask leaders to 'improve' and the tools available to help them do their job.

Chapter 7 paints a picture of the hidden lives of teachers and the diversity of their beliefs and practices. We describe how regularities emerge – habits, heuristics and routines – which enable teachers to function despite the complexity and ambiguity of their roles. The professional isolation of teachers allows diversity to persist despite attempts by school leaders and policymakers to achieve consistency and alignment. The tensions created by isolation, diversity and habitual practices can make the teacher's role perplexing, as they are frequently asked to do things that do not make much sense to them, yet they can easily assume that they are alone in feeling this. We argue that by gaining insight into the hidden lives of teachers we might support them better in their challenging role.

We begin to explore the perspective of school leaders in chapter 8 by asking what compels them to frequently and assertively instruct teachers as to how to teach. This 'interventionist identity', we argue, arises from the complexity of the school system but is often in denial of this complexity, leading to a creeping managerialism and a 'fix it' mentality.

Attempts at improvement by school leaders is considered further in chapter 9. We explore how school leaders make sense of the complex reality of their school by forming an 'imagined school' that, if they are not careful, becomes the object of their improvement efforts rather than the school itself. This imagined school is necessarily simplistic and is not beset by the fundamental problems of schooling – it is fixable! Weak feedback loops mean the illusion can remain unchallenged. We argue that school leaders must learn to countenance the diversity, ambiguity and complexity of schools if they are to avoid naïve interventions and harmful effects.

Finally, in chapter 10, we discuss the importance of stories and metaphors in our understanding of school improvement and complete our caricature of the education system as a living force that resists our attempts to change it. We draw together the themes and threads of the book to argue that school improvement is inherently complex and difficult, but not impossible if our eyes are open to this complexity. We argue for simplicity on the other side of complexity and express our hopes for a more informed approach to school improvement.

CHAPTER 1 – POWERFUL UNKNOWLEDGE

Professing themselves to be wise, they became fools.

Romans 1:22[10]

For an institution whose reason-for-being arguably centres on the pursuit of knowledge, ignorance proliferates in schools. In many aspects of our educational endeavours, we do not know what we are doing. Rather than embrace and explore this ignorance that pervades every aspect of our daily lives in education, we tend to carry on as if it were not there.

Within a classroom, much of what is happening is unknown or unknowable to the teacher. Individual pupils experience the same lesson in disparate ways, and there is no reliable proxy for working out precisely who is learning exactly what. Our ignorance scales up such that those in charge of our schools make decisions based on biased and partial versions of what is going on behind closed classroom doors. And the further we sit from the complex realities of the classroom, the more our attempts to influence schooling are mired by misunderstanding, presumption and over-simplification. Policymakers may well act in good faith, but they do so based on contrasting, oblique and shifting ideas about what schooling is for and how schools actually work.

The economist Daniel Boorstin said that 'the great menace to progress is not ignorance but the illusion of knowledge'.[11] We concur and suggest that defining and embracing our ignorance is the essential first step in improving schools. Until we accept what we do not know, our progress will be impeded. We must accept that schools are not as homogenous and predictable as some would have us believe. Surface level simplicity and similarity hides a more complex and diverse reality.

Beyond that which we can know

Modern social institutions tend to be complicated, and schools are no different. They host millions of children and thousands of adults for 39 weeks a year, each one of whom make countless tiny decisions each day that produce unique and unpredictable sets of behaviours. Few of these individuals would be able to articulate their personal mission, or how it contributes to the overall purpose of the system, which itself can never be well-articulated.

But schools are not just complicated; they are also complex social spheres of interacting agents whose behaviours are both determined by, and determine, the nature of the social system in unpredictable ways.[12] Complexity arises in educational institutions for several key reasons.[13] First, education is an *interconnected system* where actions or performance in one institution or stage will affect actions or performance in another. The pupil admissions or teacher hiring policy of one school will affect others in the locality. Changes in what we choose to teach eight-year-olds will affect institutions who serve secondary-aged children. And when we reform an individual subject's curriculum or pedagogical approach, we do not anticipate how it will spill across to daily teaching in other subjects. There may be repercussions for any single act across time and across various levels in the system, but it is not always clear exactly how events will play out or when and where consequences may emerge. It is this spontaneity and responsiveness that makes schools such a vibrant place to be.

Second, the school system is made up of individuals whose behaviours adapt to the behaviour of others and the wider system. These so-called *adaptive agents* modify their strategies in diverse ways as experience accumulates, resulting in constant flux and divergent outcomes from similar starting points. While a teacher may, for a while, promptly respond to a request to meet a reporting deadline, experience may teach them that there are no apparent consequences for other teachers who do not do so, therefore the likelihood they will continue to comply falls. By contrast, another teacher, working among more conscientious colleagues, may never feel they can risk missing deadlines. Human agents are capable of learning, and this produces a system with evolutionary characteristics such that it cannot necessarily return to past states at will.[14] What is done often cannot be undone, as what is learned is not easily unlearned. This momentum drives schools forward in a constant process of becoming.

Third, schools are complex because education is surrounded by *feedback loops*, both positive and negative. Feedback is any process where information generated by an interaction is then used for decision making or regulation practices, thereby affecting subsequent interactions.[15] Positive feedback amplifies the effect of an initial interaction, moving the system away from its current state, whereas negative feedback inhibits further effects, helping return the system to equilibrium. For example, a negative feedback loop means that a noisy class entering a classroom will prompt the teacher to exert a greater calming influence, settling the pupils down to a state in which they can be taught. Whereas a positive feedback loop results if pupils respond to low-level chatter of others by feeling it is acceptable to talk themselves, thus amplifying noise to levels where it disrupts learning. As we will see in chapter 3, positive feedback loops dominate learning processes, resulting in multiplier effects that encourage divergent outcomes.

Fourth, schooling has layers of sub-systems *nested* within systems, from the child's brain to the classroom to the school to the schooling system. Insights might be gained by examining interaction *between* sub-systems, as well as those *within* systems. For example, we may be interested to know more about the inner workings of the mind (through research in cognitive psychology), and we may also explore how these minds interact in the social environment of the classroom. Similarly, we may theorise about how schools improve individually, while also observing the mechanisms for how schools compete, collaborate and adapt to the marketplace. There are insights to be gained both by studying one component sub-system in isolation and the interplay between these component systems. And beyond schooling, the education system is nested within other social systems and is necessarily related to the health and social care sector, social and cultural dynamics in family life, economic performance, and politics. The boundary between education and other systems, for example where the education system ends and social services responsibilities begin, is blurry and constantly shifting over time. Schools are shaped by wider shifts in society; for example, schools have always been places where children go so that parents can get on with adult life, but especially so since social change has altered the working lives of mothers. The porous boundaries of the schooling system mean that there is a constant interplay between schools and the wider society. Schools are both changed by the world and are significant enough to exert an influence too over the wider society.

Finally, complexity arises as educational change emerges over decades rather than hours. We will only observe the full impact of a primary teacher's long-term sickness on their class (or indeed a pandemic on a generation) years later. The national curriculum is substantially reformed with each political cycle, yet we can only learn how reforms affected the children who experienced them long after those reforms were abandoned and replaced by something new. We respond to the immediate and visible signs of our success but are blind to the long-term implications of our actions.

The inherent complexity of the schooling system means we know far less than we would like to about how schools function and about the impact of our attempts to change them. Establishing cause-and-effect relationships under complexity is necessarily difficult. We are forced to simplify, collectively ascribing attributes to the emergent behaviour of groups of individuals in the system – a department, the teaching staff, the year group – as though these groups act together with purpose.

This description of our complex educational system may make us feel uncomfortable, for it cannot be controlled by a central planner. But complex social systems have many positive attributes, such as the capacity for self-organisation. Complex systems are constantly evolving, able to meet the changing needs of society without annual legislative change to determine how they should operate. Teachers within schools spontaneously come together to create valuable experiences for students, without the need for central direction or a plan from the Secretary of State. They respond to the ad hoc needs of individual students in ways that can never be codified. Teachers can adapt to the environment of a new school, without any need for formal re-training. The scientist

Richard Cook says that complex systems are always flawed, always operating in a slightly degraded mode because they are too complex to ever optimise and run perfectly.[16] However, their complexity also tends to make them quite resilient to catastrophe. Despite constant errors and failures (and barring a pandemic), school life goes on, day after day, in thousands of institutions.

Unquestioned regularities

Our state of ignorance – as teachers, as leaders, as policymakers – is inevitable, given the complexity of the system we inhabit, the opaqueness of its output and intractability of the challenges it is set to solve. Working in education we are constantly called upon to face up to ignorance and uncertainty, navigating our daily lives in schools regardless. If you think hard about the complexity of the system, it is natural to wonder how it is possible that the gates to schools across the world open every morning at all. And why is the classroom teacher not paralysed by indecision as each class begins?

The only reason we can work so effortlessly despite our ignorance is the presence of well-established *procedural regularities* that facilitate actions without the need to question or engage in nuance and ambiguity. Procedural and behavioural regularities constitute the fabric of daily life in our schools. They are 'the way we do things around here' and generally go without saying. The school bell marks out the transitions between place and activity. Pupils move in an orderly way towards their next destination, then sit in their designated or habitual place, to experience a lesson that likely looks and feels very much like the last. We teach the curriculum in roughly the same well-defined subjects that we always have, punctuated by end-of-year tests that persist in a similar form, even as their official purpose changes. Pupils behave, and misbehave, according to social norms encouraged by the school or dictated by the pupils. Terms start and end, pupils and staff come and go, and we rarely look down at the tracks that guide our thought and action.

Regularities generally emerge over time and often there is no institutional memory of how or why they are the way they are (although there may be an acceptable narrative that it is convenient to believe). No scholar has ever written the history of morning registration or exercise book use. Regularities are rarely designed and built, even less frequently rebuilt, from first principles. Schools rely on teachers, students and parents sharing a broadly similar expectation and acceptance of the basic grammar of school life. Regularities are the habits and routines that give schools their internal momentum and we disrupt them at our peril.

Of course, not all decisions in schools are habituated and sometimes we must make explicit decisions. For these we tend to ignore complexity and ignorance by utilising basic decision frames (or simple maps) with which we are comfortable, or that are considered the norm. We follow a flow chart to guide us as to whether we should report a safeguarding concern. We use an end-of-term test to decide which ability groups children belong in. We present options for change as either/or decisions, accompanied by stylised lists of pros and cons. We weigh up the differing views of stakeholders and decree which group's preferences should guide our decisions. Together, simple decision frames and regularities spare us the need to countenance the intractable complexity at the heart of schooling. Much of the time we do not want to be troubled by the messiness of reality, and the system may not benefit from us being distracted by it either.

The success of procedural regularities and rules of thumb (or heuristics) in helping us operate without being overcome by the complexity of decision making is such that we find it hard to question *why* things are the way they are. We often suffer from social amnesia, a collective forgetting about how (and even why) now 'normal' social practices once came to be. Forgetting leads to social constructions becoming accepted as concrete reality, a process called reification. Within schools both processes occur in relation to procedural regularities. If we once knew, or acted differently, we have forgotten. Ben vividly remembers his first parents' evening, sat in the hall staring at three empty chairs nervously awaiting his first five-minute appointment. He took the opportunity to ask the teachers positioned around him: 'What are we aiming to achieve here?' Despite having decades of teaching experience between them, not one could provide a clear answer. We will undoubtedly all have such stories, when simply asking 'why?' is met with blank faces.

Even those teachers who claim that schools are overly regulated institutions that stifle individual freedom of expression would accept that regularities are often necessary and beneficial. Indeed, the most harmful attempts to improve schools have often been guilty of ignoring or underestimating the benefits of the status quo. The existence of these procedural regularities in our collective consciousness affords schools the capacity to orchestrate the daily behaviours of hundreds of individual children and adults. Students and teachers expect timetables with a daily carousel of fixed-length lessons in discrete subjects, assemblies, lunch and break times and the occasional detention. Students and their parents expect about 13 academic years of this experience shared with a cohort born within 12 months of one another. These regularities have emerged for a reason and often enable the system to function in ways we do not fully understand. The system is wiser than we are, and we should attempt to understand its patterns and emergent behaviours before we disrupt them.

Messy reality

This poorly understood complexity of the education system presents a dilemma for those charged with running and improving schools, for if they were to truly appreciate how complex the task ahead of them was, they would never dare change anything. And yet they do make changes, usually falling back on simple frames of reference that do not touch upon complexity. Humans have a natural tendency to believe that they can fix problems and make things better. The idea that some problems in education are fundamental and so intractable is inconceivable to most. They dare not countenance that all leadership actions are gambles – acts that necessarily take place in the face of uncertainty. People seek comfort in searching for patterns and coherence in what they see, feel, think and do. It is pragmatic to pretend to know what is unknowable, to assume commonality where there is diversity, to second-guess the motivations of others, to confidently predict the unpredictable, to claim causal relationships that are (in reality) far looser than we would like and to quantify and codify the unmeasurable. This tendency is revealed in the linear certainty of school development plans, the tick-box lesson observation records, post hoc rationalisation of events, 'non-negotiables' and data analysis. Out of simple narratives of how schools work and grand plans for what they can deliver come naïve expectations. The dissonance between these naïve expectations and the more complex reality inevitably produces tensions.

Given this complexity, perhaps it is inevitable that our thinking about education is fuzzy, changeable and subject to fashions. No single expert or disciplinary perspective will ever manage to make sense of this education system we all care so deeply about. 'Expertise' takes on a different meaning in conditions of uncertainty: rather than knowing all there is to know, expertise becomes the ability to 'describe a problematic situation in a way that supports wise action'.[17] Perhaps the ability to hold one's ideas lightly has value in such a system, and the ability to change one's mind an essential quality. If an expert expresses certainty about the cause of problems or claims they can predict the future, then this is a good indicator that they are not to be trusted.

Education is subject to so much reform by people who aspire for the system to be something that it is not, and yet so much remains the same regardless. Everything changes. Simultaneously, very little does. Our children are receiving an education that feels remarkably like the one that we had as children. Long-run studies of educational attainment by Professor Rob Coe and others suggest that the amount that is learned in childhood has not changed very much over the past few decades.[18] The determinants of socioeconomic gaps in attainment remain as intransient as ever. Sometimes it feels like the education system is a creature with a life of its own that defies our attempts to manipulate it. Explaining this juxtaposition of change yet stability, of reform yet permanence, is central to this book.

Becoming unknowledgeable

We contend that educators working with and within schools often do not appreciate how much they do not know. Rather than continue in denial of our ignorance, this book argues that we must first accept it, and then define it. Like the early cartographers seeking to chart unexplored territories, we invite readers to seek out the *terra incognita* in schooling. As we locate and acknowledge these unmapped regions in our understanding, we will transform our ignorance into 'unknowledge' – a well-defined, yet unexplored, part of our knowledge-map.[19]

By setting out exactly what we do not know – our unknowledge of schooling – we are primed to explore it rather than to ignore it. While this exploration will make us individually more knowledgeable, even if we chose to spend a lifetime studying schooling, we would still not reach every corner of our own unknowledge. There are some regions of unknowledge that are completely out of reach to all, either now or forever. For example, we may never know how individual neurons create networks that produce the phenomenon of knowing about magnetic energy. Other regions are known by someone in the system, but we are not clear who holds which cards. The scattered intelligence of a schooling system designed around the personal, tacit knowledge of its members makes individuals all the more ignorant when confronted with a dilemma that requires this collective wisdom.

Our unknowledge may be why, as individuals working within or upon the system, from time to time we feel lost. The individual frames of reference (or map) that we use to locate ourselves, to understand our role and to inform our actions fails to correspond to a rather messier reality. We diligently follow our maps, look up and realise we are not where they tell us we should be.

Most teachers and leaders will have experienced moments where they are confronted with the paucity of a single working model for adequately explaining what transpires in a school. This may often be observed in new senior leaders who design sleek systems that they believe will be followed by all and deliver greater efficiency, only to discover that the old, imperfect system had the benefit that people understood it and used it consistently. We might ignore this dissonance and desperately double-down on the same actions. We might resign ourselves (literally or mentally) to the futility of our efforts. Or we might adopt a new map and try again. The fact that so few succumb to resignation about the transient effect of their actions is testament to our enduring belief that the desired destination is both a worthy, and an attainable one. If our past efforts failed, then we must simply try harder this time.

Such epiphanies also periodically occur at scale, provoked by a growing, widespread and unavoidable realisation that what once seemed like an obvious solution or way of improving schools has failed to work as hoped. However, though smaller narratives can be discarded, the more enduring beliefs in the power of mass schooling to transform society live on, producing the ever-lasting search for a new policy tool, for the Next Big Thing to improve schools.

Once in a generation a catastrophic event, such as a war or a pandemic, casts the regularities of the school in a new light as the natural rhythms of events, processes and systems that normally continue without scrutiny are suddenly disrupted. Pale imitations of these regularities can be quickly created, but the difficulties in doing so only add further to the dissonant effect of pausing everything we take for granted. It leads to unveiling of our own ideology, biases and assumptions as we struggle to give meaning to that previously hidden in plain sight. Perhaps it is only when schools close their doors that we can start to make sense of why they exist at all.

We may not be able to handle too much reality. Day-to-day existence and even simple decision making may not be enhanced by continually contemplating the provisional nature of all that appears concrete, simple and necessary. However, in this book we argue for embracing the messiness of reality more, especially when making strategic decisions intended to shape what happens within our schools. We also argue that it is right that we question our mental maps and not allow them to become too rigid or egocentric. We are naturally drawn to narratives in which we are the hero – where the solution is by coincidence within our power, remit and skillset. By accepting that there are other, equally valid, versions of the story we may avoid the worst excesses of this tendency.

The transformation of ignorance into unknowledge will make our efforts to understand schooling more productive and our decisions wiser. We may reduce the strain and dissonance experienced when naïve maps clash with the complex reality of the world we inhabit. As we inch forward a little more unknowledgeable than we were before, aware of the gaps in our understanding and cognisant of our uncertainties, so we can seek to avoid acting upon naïve ideas about what schools are and what they can achieve. We will dampen our temptation to misdiagnose the nature of the problems we face. Indeed, we might feel better equipped to tackle some problems.

If you feel that our assessment of the schooling system is downbeat, we beg to differ. There is nothing to be gained by pretending that schools are simple, fully explainable and entirely within our control. On the contrary, an honest appraisal of our certainty and influence should enhance our appreciation of how precious our time and energy is; how it is not to be wasted on futile, ill-informed gestures at change. If the school system sometimes perplexes us that is because it is perplexing. We should not be cowed by this. Improving schools is hard; why pretend otherwise?

So, with humility and gallantry, let us confront the intractable problems that are at the heart of education.

Complex advice

By acknowledging our unknowledge and the complexity of the education system, there is a risk we feel powerless and confused. However, by embracing the messy and imperfect reality of schools, we may find new ways to make sense of some of the peculiar, frustrating and perplexing things we experience.

To navigate our way through uncertainty and ignorance, we suggest the following:

1. Be clear about what you do not know and accept what you will never fully know.
2. Accept that what is known is mostly in the minds of others, so work hard to harness their wisdom.
3. See yourself as part of a complex, interconnected system. Accept that what happens is largely not within your control.
4. Observe procedural regularities and consider what purpose they perform. Learn what you can about the history of regularities in your school and why they emerged in the first place. Think carefully before you dismantle them.

Reflective questions

- To what extent does Daniel Boorstin's claim that 'the great menace to progress is not ignorance but the illusion of knowledge' apply to schools?
- What are the domains of unknowledge for you personally? Is it possible to define these?
- Do you recognise the depiction of schools as part of a complex social system? What are the implications for the work that you do in relation to schools?
- Can you think of a reified procedural regularity that exists for unknown reasons?
- Can you think of a procedural regularity that has been recently disrupted? Was this disruption intentional or accidental? What were the consequences of this?
- Do you recall reaching a realisation that what once seemed like an obvious solution or way of improving schools has failed to work as hoped?

CHAPTER 2 – MAPPING THE TERRITORY

> *Our view of reality is like a map with which to negotiate the terrain of life. If the map is true and accurate ... we will generally know how to get there. If the map is false and inaccurate, we generally will be lost.*
>
> M. Scott Peck, *The Road Less Traveled*[20]

Joseph Mayer Rice was on a mission. He was determined to stamp out 'narrow, tedious and mechanical' teaching practices from American schools using the methods of the embryonic field of educational research. A physician and son of German immigrants, Rice had learned of the revolutionary ideas of experimentation and measuring the mind on a two-year visit to Germany in 1888–90.[21]

Writing in *Scientific Management in Education*, Rice despaired at 'uncertainty and indefiniteness' in the field of education:

> *We have opinions innumerable, but no facts are at hand in support of our opinions. Educators are divided into creeds; and while the members of the same creed are frequently in harmony with one another, and sometimes form a mutual admiration society, there are few points on which the different creeds themselves agree.*[22]

Rice believed the gains of a scientific approach to schooling would allow the creation of a genuine teaching profession with common standards and approaches that maximised the efficiency of children's learning. He set about conducting one of the first ever comparative tests of thousands of American children, using the data to discover 'what works' in schooling. The charting of the unknown regions of educational ignorance had begun. Alongside other pioneers in the field, Rice contributed to the development of new procedures and methods for measuring the mind. These founding researchers urged teachers to undertake research and promoted the formation of research organisations. The frenzy of pre-World War II activity was enormous – from 1918 to 1927 alone, Monroe found 3650 articles to include in his bibliography of educational research.[23]

Among Rice's first findings was the assertion that there was no relationship between time spent learning spellings via drills in class and spelling test performance.[24] This absence of a hypothesised relationship is called a null effect and it was the first of many that would be discovered by educational researchers. While the implications of a null effect appear obvious on the surface – it is not worth doing the thing in question – in reality, their interpretation goes to the heart of trying to understand why map making is so difficult in education.

Medieval maps

A century after the work of Joseph Mayer Rice, a New Zealand-Australian academic called John Hattie decided to compile the map of educational best practice. His book, *Visible Learning*,[25] is a league table of good things to do in schools, collating quantitative studies and scoring the effectiveness of interventions. In theory, this was a compelling approach for teachers, gifting them a neat and transparent means of deciding which innovations were worth trying and which were not. In practice, the map was unfortunately more akin to a medieval than a modern Ordnance Survey one: incomplete, lacking in detail and downright incorrect in places.

Blame for the inadequacy of the map does not lie with John Hattie, but rather with the inherently weak evidence base in education. Take, for example, the thing at the top of Hattie's list: feedback. Hattie's map claimed that feedback would accelerate the pace of learning more than other interventions. After Visible Learning became popular, schools duly set about doing a lot of it. Unfortunately, John Hattie's map did not tell school leaders exactly what feedback should look like in their school. It was used as a justification for more marking, more prescriptive marking policies, more questioning techniques in class, more group feedback, more individualised feedback and so on. It took a long time for educational researchers to dig deeply into the basis on which feedback was deemed to be an effective intervention. Few teachers had any idea that the original research had focused on whether feedback could alter behaviours, not learning. They might also have been surprised to know that only a tiny proportion of the research was carried out in schools.[26]

The doubtful collation of disparate studies of school practice was not the only reason why dissenters began to criticise these maps or toolkits of 'what works'.[27] Statisticians pointed out that the calculation of impact on learning is not straightforwardly comparable across studies, since effect sizes have a tendency to be larger in smaller studies on targeted students that measure immediate outcomes that are highly aligned to the intervention.[28]

Perhaps most importantly, there are many areas of largely uncharted or roughly sketched territory that could not be included in the map. Take, for example, marking – an enormous daily activity undertaken by teachers. The Education Endowment Foundation (EEF) (introduced below) had also gotten into map making and duly commissioned a research team to report back on what existing evidence said about how teachers should mark. The 35-page report gives a clear answer: we do not know.[29] Research also tells us almost nothing about the other huge part of a teacher's job: lesson planning. For example, we do not know whether teachers who plan their own lessons are then able to teach more effective classes than those teachers who are gifted a lesson plan.

You may wonder how, in more than a century of educational research, we have managed to say so little about what the map of effective educational practice looks like. One reason is that for much of this time in the post-Second World War era, the pendulum of educational research had swung away from quantitative and experimental research towards qualitative and phenomenological approaches. As a result, only a small proportion of researchers were contributing to map-making by trying to make causal assertions about whether a policy or practice could improve attainment. It seems that not even scholarly activity in education is immune from the Next Big Thing!

The modern mapmakers

It took a new century to bring about another revolution in educational map-making. In England in the early 2010s, the medic and academic Ben Goldacre was brought in by the government to explain how the revolution that scientific methods have brought to medicine were a 'huge prize waiting to be claimed by teachers'.[30] At about the same time, the coalition government created the aforementioned Education Endowment Foundation, which would run randomised controlled trials to tell us how to close the attainment gap. Once again, this 'what works' movement placed fixed design, quantitative research at the forefront of policy making. Finally, statisticians would be able to tell people how to run schools and how to teach!

On the face of it, randomised controlled trials would seem to be essential in an industry such as education where the generation of learning is so complex and therefore subject to confounding explanations, as we will show in the next chapter. The intelligence they generate should guide school leaders who struggle with more ad hoc trial-and-error approaches to improving their school, as we will discuss in chapters 8 and 9. Randomised controlled trials claim to override the complexity problem in schools by isolating a single thing to test – whether a product, a pedagogic practice or a school policy approach – while holding everything else 'constant'. And by observing the phenomenon at scale, across multiple schools, these trials can measure average differences in outcomes between the schools who receive the treatment and those continuing 'business as normal', even if the participating schools are really rather diverse.

Over the past decade, the Education Endowment Foundation has run more than 190 trials involving more than half of all schools in England and more than one million students. And yet, if a classroom teacher were to read the hundreds of trial reports to gain insights as to how to teach better, or a school leader were to read them in the hope of improving their management approach, they would be sorely disappointed. And the reason for their disappointment, above all others, would simply be that most documents report a null effect. In other words, they report that the trialled intervention was no better than 'business as normal' in schools.

Things that seemed to be no better than 'business as normal' include incentive payments to students for effort in class and homework, peer tutoring in primary maths, playing chess in primary schools, parental engagement programmes, growth mindset sessions, behavioural support to students at risk of exclusion, a one-to-one literacy intervention, online maths tuition and a computer-based phonics intervention.[31]

When Rice found a null effect in his study of spelling, he concluded that spelling drills didn't work. However, his conclusion might have been premature, for null effects can appear for a variety of reasons. Poor research design can produce erroneous null effects. Some argue that it is possible that many of the ideas about how to improve learning that were trialled by the Education Endowment Foundation *could* have been effective, but the research design did not facilitate this and instead produced 'false negatives'. Researchers from Loughborough showed that many of these trials were not run at a large enough scale to be able to identify whether they worked or not, especially for students from disadvantaged backgrounds.[32] Too small, or underpowered, trials are a problem across the social sciences.[33] But even for very large trials – known as effectiveness trials – results have been quite disappointing. For the 28 primary school effectiveness trials that were run at scale because the Education Endowment Foundation already had prior evidence that they were likely to prove to be worthwhile, just nine produced a positive impact.[34]

We may ask whether English researchers are just not very good at running research projects at scale, but similar approaches in other countries appear to generate disappointing outcomes, too.[35] Perhaps we should face up to the fact that most educational interventions do not work that well: at least not universally, or in isolation.

Complex systems need time

It is possible that complexity, rather than simply 'false negatives', is the best explanation for why few trials appear to improve outcomes. In other words, they *truly* did not work out well for the schools who took part in the trial. Education scientists are forced to labour under the kind of lab conditions that purer scientists would find intolerable with messy 'labs', non-blinded participants and uncontrollable control groups.[36] Each of these trials must be implemented into a complex schooling system, with diverse teachers, pupils and schools, all with unique circumstances and interacting in unpredictable ways with the programme.

The rules of a randomised controlled trial say we must take a fixed blueprint for a programme and implement it overnight so that we can measure its effectiveness within a year or two. It allows no time to experiment, train and work out how to align a new programme with a school or a classroom. We know that asking teachers to change their practice is very difficult because they rely so heavily on automated behaviours that are hard to disrupt, even if the will is there (a phenomenon we explore in chapter 7). Given the complexity of the school system, it is understandable that the pipeline from the blueprint of the intervention to the implementation in schools has multiple fractures.[37] In research reports published following these null effect findings, researchers often describe this fractured pipeline as 'implementation problems' or 'low engagement', viewing this as a failure of the schools who took part rather than the programme itself. They fail to recognise that the 'intervention' and the 'implementation' are one and the same. In the words of teacher Adam Boxer, 'if something is very difficult to implement, it's not a good intervention'.[38] Or rather, it could be a good idea, but teachers need years rather than months to incorporate and refine the programme in their classroom.

Complexity and divergence

Complexity means we might have an implementation problem when it comes to trials. In other words, they *can* be used to identify the average effect of an intervention, but the trials simply need to be allowed to run for a longer length of time. However, complexity might also cause interventions to have an unpredictable and indeterminate effect on schools. Implementation of change within a school requires dozens of inter-dependent bodies to move in the manner intended. In the 19th century, Poincaré showed that even with just three heavenly bodies that are interdependent, movements start to look chaotic and unpredictable.[39] Schools have more than three interdependent bodies! Therefore, the outcomes of school improvement initiatives are likely to be highly sensitive to initial conditions and behaviours in the school.

If schools have divergent responses to interventions, then *average* 'effects' of interventions that are estimated for the schools that took part tell us little about whether the effect is likely to be positive in a particular school. If a maths mastery programme was shown to work, on average, for the schools taking part in the trial, what does that mean if a leader tries to implement it in their school? Furthermore, if something was shown to be effective in one trial and ineffective in another (as was the case for the Grammar for Writing programme), which trial should we all trust?[40] If an intervention was shown to work on an older age group but not a younger age group, but gives no explanation as to why, should we take this as evidence of a differential age effect or simply chance differences? And in the most serious cases, if a trial shows that a programme lowers student attainment, which the Achievement for All trial seemed to do, should I withdraw from the Achievement for All programme even if I personally believe my school's participation is worthwhile?[41]

The sensitivity of the impact of an intervention to the exact conditions under which it is implemented helps explain why researchers are likely to find it difficult to replicate previous findings. We know from the psychology reproducibility project, for example, that only 39% of experiments in their field replicated.[42] In our own education field, replication of experiments is extremely uncommon, representing just 0.13% of articles published in top journals. Of the tiny number of replications in education, just half were successful.[43]

Randomised controlled trials are great vehicles for model testing, providing a clear framework as to when a model should be replaced with a new one.[44] However, in education they are rarely used in this way. This is largely because stable theoretical models are rather lacking in education, which unavoidably relies on multiple social science disciplines to make sense of schooling. We are forced to design research based on poorly developed conceptions of how students learn, how teachers teach and how schools are run. As a result, we take a 'black box' approach of asking whether the intervention 'works', without testing the individual theories that make up the plausible mechanism by which it could work. We saw this with Rice, who was simply interested in whether there was a correlation between time spent on spelling drills and test performance; he did not seek to find evidence for competing theories of what happens in the mind when children learn to spell. As a result, he also struggled to explain why the null effect was found.

We have three plausible explanations for a null effect following a trial:

1. The intervention doesn't work; it is no better than existing practice.
2. The intervention could be made to work, but the trial was inadequately set up or run over too short a time to cope with complex adaptation to the programme.
3. Complexity means that declaring the intervention as one that 'works' or 'doesn't work' is futile because its impact is unpredictable and highly diverse across schools, depending on their exact conditions.

It matters to researchers which explanation best fits each null effect found because it allows us to use null findings to build knowledge and refine future research. Correctly interpreting the null effect matters to schools because it determines how they incorporate the information into the map used to navigate school improvement.

Complex trials

As a knowledge-building technology, randomised controlled trials remain one of the least flawed approaches we have. The Education Endowment Foundation has done so much to raise the standards of good practice in implementing trials by requiring pre-registration of methods and submission of coding and analysis.[45] We believe that there *are* still many under-researched areas of school practice that are amenable to being trialled because they are likely to have a reasonably consistent impact across schools. For example, England has converged on relatively consistent practice around the teaching of phonetic decoding. We see no reason why we should not develop a stronger evidence base around instruction of handwriting, spelling, grammar and maths. But if we are to run trials in these areas, giving plausibly useful interventions the chance to show their value means doing trials in a way that recognises schools and teachers as living entities that adapt and morph practice around the interventions that we try to impose on them.

It was health and medicine academics who persuaded education officials that randomised controlled trials should be used for knowledge building in education. And, once again, it is academics who have struggled with making healthcare interventions work in practice that can teach us a great deal about how to run trials in complex settings.[46] We need to move away from the idea that a programme blueprint can be blithely imposed on schools and consider the principles of Holly Lanham and her colleagues who recommend considering the following when planning interventions in complex settings: first, we should acknowledge unpredictability. Interventions in schools will not have a single, deterministic effect on the teachers and pupils. Second, we should recognise the self-organising characteristic of complex systems and account for this by modifying interventions accordingly. Third, we should expect, and seek to learn about, interdependencies between different parts of the system. And lastly, we should encourage teachers and pupils to make sense of what is changing: to ask questions, admit ignorance, explore paradoxes and reflect collectively.

To understand how programmes evolve in complex settings, we might need to run even larger trials with multiple arms, each allowing the intervention to be run in a slightly different way.[47] At each stage, money needs to be spent measuring exactly how the trial is evolving and what is happening, for it is only then that we can see how behaviours match up to our theoretical models. We must allow trials to run over a period within which change is possible. In the case of schools, this is almost never days, and it is rarely terms; it is usually years. Ideally trials would not just learn something about average effectiveness across schools taking part, for no school is 'average'. Instead, it would also ideally learn something about the 'boundary conditions', beyond which the intervention is likely to be unsuccessful. These boundary conditions could be anything from curriculum subject, age of child, preferred pedagogy of teacher, experiences of teaching staff or social context of school.

The Oxford academic Trisha Greenhalgh, who has also written extensively about the use of randomised controlled trials in social settings, urges us not to dismiss their use in complex social interventions, but rather to recognise that, just as observational studies often overestimate the effect of an educational intervention, the trial is constructed such that it is likely to underestimate it.[48] She suggests we recognise a more organic model of causality with multiple interacting influences. We should therefore stop asking, 'What is the effect and is it statistically significant?' and instead ask, 'Does this intervention contribute to a better outcome?' This approach recognises that multiple interventions might each contribute to an overall beneficial effect, even though none of these interventions individually would have a statistically significant impact on any predefined variable.

Shifting terrain

One reason we draw maps is so that we can navigate our way from one place to another. Knowing what the terrain looks like allows us to choose a starting point and a destination, and to be prepared with the equipment we need. If our educational maps are to be useful, they must serve these purposes for teachers in their classrooms. However, what if the terrain is substantially different for each teacher or even for each of their individual students? And what if this terrain changes each time the teacher sets out on their journey? What of teachers' disparate beliefs regarding where they aspire to navigate their class to, and the most effective means of leading them there? Two factors – diversity and change – threaten to undermine map-making efforts that rely on a degree of commonality and stability.

Diversity is a problem for developing a shared understanding of 'what works'. What research seeks to establish is technologies that work everywhere, or at least in enough contexts to make them a good bet. But what if teaching is about the particular more than the universal? We may find that what works in one classroom or school does not travel to a new context. We may learn that establishing good practice rules that standardise practice across classrooms is suboptimal – that allowing diversity to flourish is optimal.

Unpredictability and diversity are uncomfortable to those seeking to understand how the educational system works. They undermine the scientific project that attempts to establish rules about what works. They explain why educational researchers in the mid-20th century, frustrated with scientific progress in modelling the system, swung back towards more qualitative approaches that could focus on the particular rather than the general. These calls for new approaches to research never go away, even where scientific approaches are in the ascendency, but they do not provide the kind of answers we crave since they have equally poor technologies for improvement.[49] For while they attempt to develop local solutions that make sense for one school's given context, dealing with the inherent nuance and complexity of instructional practices, without better theories or maps they too have no framework for asserting whether a solution would travel to any other school. The shrinking of the domain of unknowledge is painfully slow, leaving space for Next Big Things to flourish.

While we believe that there are unmapped parts of the terrain that are stable and consistent enough to document, we suspect the toolkit of 'what works' in school improvement can never be fully completed. What should we do in these circumstances? The philosopher Nancy Cartwright, who has studied evidence gathering in complex social policy fields, offers some rules of thumb that can be used with the aim of developing what might be thought of as compromised theoretical models, but she more positively calls 'ex ante case-specific causal models'.[50] 'Ex ante' because they are for before-the-fact prediction of what the likely effects of proposed actions are. In other words, they can help school leaders predict what is likely to happen in their school. 'Case-specific' because they are not concerned with studies that provide evidence for some general conclusion but rather with using what general and local knowledge one can get to predict what will happen to a specific school in their real-life setting. 'Causal' because using case studies they aim to trace out as best as possible the web of causal processes that will be responsible for what happens. Nancy Cartwright's argument that we should aim to closely study ex ante case-specific causal models is a good one, but it is only really feasible for narrow or small-scale interventions. To take the example of two large-scale trials that the Education Endowment Foundation has run, we could plausibly use her approach to develop a causal model of how a breakfast club might lead to improved attainment in a setting, but it would be infeasible to use her approach to evidence causal mechanisms for a generic school improvement approach such as Achievement for All.

Elusive maps

This chapter has sounded a note of caution about our enthusiasm for making maps in education. We do know more about what will work in our schools than we did a decade (or a century) ago, but the evidence-based journey has been slower and harder than anyone expected. We have poor maps to navigate school improvement, but worse than this, we have poor technologies for making better maps and a landscape that is not very amenable to being charted. To some extent we cannot avoid the fact that even high-level regularities of things that 'tend to work', on average, may look rather unpredictable and messy within any individual classroom. We shouldn't beat ourselves up about this since other professions face the same issues. For example, in medicine we do not know why even the most effective drugs fail to work on large numbers of people with the condition they are supposed to treat.[51] Bodies, like social systems, are complex.

There are always glimmers of hope – new intelligence about what teachers should do in the classroom. For example, in 2020 a meta-analysis of retrieval practice was able to show teachers how effectively testing can enhance the long-term retention of studied knowledge.[52] It not only showed what type of environment conditions were associated with effective use of testing but gave support for three theories to explain the effect (additional exposure, transfer-appropriate processing and motivation). That said, even this review doesn't give teachers instructions as to how to use testing in the classroom. It doesn't provide a GCSE history teacher, for example, with a proven route to success, though it does provide clues about how to travel there a little more effectively. Furthermore, given that testing is one of the most heavily researched parts of cognitive science with typical effect sizes that are much larger than for other mechanisms, we are relatively sceptical that a similar quality of evidence on other instructional tools such as interleaving, spacing or dual coding will appear any time soon.[53] We hope we will be proved wrong.

Joseph Mayer Rice understood some of these issues with as much clarity as we have today. He wrote:

> *It may be that the nature of the child's mind is so elusive, and the influence of natural endowment, heredity, and environment so varied, that all definite observation is rendered impossible. Or, on the other hand, it may be that we have not yet applied the proper methods of observation. If the former is true, we shall have to abandon the idea of ever developing a real science of pedagogy, and continue to grope our way in the dark. If, on the other hand, the latter is the case, then we must see what can be done to improve our methods of observation.*[54]

Joseph Mayer Rice was a pioneer in the field of educational research, and we owe him a great deal for nudging us towards a scientific approach to school improvement. We wonder how he would feel were he able to see the continuing state of our unknowledge today. He must have felt his own research on spelling had nicely filled in the map of what works, yet the education community seemingly felt otherwise. In 2021, psychologists Steven Pan, Timothy Rickard and Robert Bjork wrote a review on whether and how spelling should be taught in schools, summarising the hundreds of research studies that have been published since Rice's 1898 study.[55] Twelve decades after Rice, there is still no consensus on what the map of spelling instruction looks like. It isn't that we've made no progress, but rather that we've learned that instruction of even something as simple as spelling is…well…complex!

The consequence of our unknowledge is that teachers across English-speaking classrooms use hundreds of diverse approaches to teach spelling to young children. This diversity in the choices that teachers make may be justified, given the complexity of the challenges of the classroom and the fundamental problems they face in ensuring that all children are able to learn. It is to these fundamental problems of the classroom we turn in the next chapter.

Complex advice

Schools are part of a complex environment that makes research difficult. As a result, the maps we use to choose our school improvement journeys are partial and unreliable.

To use our maps appropriately, we suggest the following:

1. Be cautious about school claims of effective practice or researcher claims that a programme 'works'. Is the apparent success real, and do you understand the causal mechanisms by which good practice is produced?
2. Take the time to question the theoretical model on which research is based (if, indeed, there is one).
3. Focus interventions on well-defined, discrete deficiencies that can be isolated, the improvement of which is aligned to your organisation's aims, and for which improvement is knowable within reasonable time scales.
4. Consider more than what research says about the effect of an intervention before adopting or abandoning it. What works or does not work elsewhere, or on average, may not be a good indicator of potential efficacy in your context.

Reflective questions

- How much attention is paid in schools, in your experience, to ascertaining the effect of improvement efforts?
- To what extent do school improvement efforts acknowledge the complexity of schools?
- Try to imagine introducing a new programme into your school or classroom. What would have to change and adapt for the programme to be a success?
- Think of some recent school improvement efforts that you have been involved in. Were they 'black box' approaches (concerned with what works, rather than why it works) or was there a clear theoretical model underpinning their adoption? If the latter, how does this model look now, with the benefit of hindsight?

CHAPTER 3 – YOU SHOULD KNOW THIS

> *I really hate it when teachers say things like: 'you should know this' or 'this is Year Seven work' or 'this was in your Key Stage 3 textbook'. It makes me feel even more pathetic than I already am!*
>
> A Year 9 student taking part in a focus group

A student wrote the quote above in response to the question: 'What would it be helpful for your teachers to understand about your experiences in their lessons?' They were a participant in one of Ben's focus groups that he hosted across three secondary schools, where he found that this type of sentiment was more commonly expressed than any other. Wanting to understand more, through further conversations with teachers and students, Ben learned that the words 'You Should Know This' were typically uttered as part of the following common sequence to open a lesson.

First, the teacher finds that some students do not know what they should in order for the planned lesson to work. This leads them to tell the class, 'You Should Know This' (or words to that effect). They may illustrate this point by reminding students of when they 'learned' it. The teacher then proceeds to teach the class as if they did know 'this', despite having just established that some students did not.

Most teachers will reluctantly admit that they have expressed the 'You Should Know This' sentiment with their own classes. They do so reluctantly, because it represents a point of failure in the accepted model of schooling whereby students arrive in a lesson with some relevant prior knowledge, are taught the lesson that can only be understood because this prior knowledge is secure and so leave the class more knowledgeable and ready to move on to the next lesson.

What they will not admit is that this is a point of *inevitable* failure in mass schooling. The inevitable failure that results in teachers repeatedly executing the 'You Should Know This' routine in class arises due to the two fundamental problems of schooling. These are:

1. Learning is invisible and cannot ever be fully known and measured by teachers.
2. Students in a typical class have inevitably diverse knowledge and capabilities, yet must all move together through the curriculum in lock-step fashion.

Teaching in the dark

The art of teaching appears simple on the surface. We invoke the language of transportation to task teachers with moving groups of students' learning forward in a consistent and uniform manner. We talk about students 'moving on' to a new topic, 'making progress', 'developing', 'advancing' or 'moving up a flight path of attainment'.

These metaphors mask the reality that the classroom is permeated with unknowledge. We teach in the dark, not fully knowing what each student knew before the lesson, nor what they know afterwards. We believe we are trying to build upon interconnected knowledge structures inside students' heads, but we are not sure what they should look like and where the interdependencies between knowledge lie. Moreover, we suspect that knowledge structures are not linear, so our metaphors of movement are vast oversimplifications.

Learning is invisible and intangible, and there is limited consensus on what it is or quite how to effect it. Educational neuroscience is still in its infancy, studying the most complex of our organs, which has at least eight systems interacting with one another. It is possible that each of these systems may have entirely different preferred ways of learning, of interacting with other systems, of forgetting and so on.[56] Neuroscience tells us that learning arises because neurons exchange chemical and electronic signals through a network, which is constantly changing and evolving as we encounter life experiences. Learning is therefore probably best described as changing the strength of connections between neurons. Of course, we cannot yet see individual neurons firing and wiring, and are even further away from a theory of consciousness or cross-brain processing. For now, at least, the brain remains one of the 'enduring mysteries of science'.[57]

The brain is a complex system because the network of neurons is constantly interacting and evolving. The consequences of these interactions are the emergent behaviours and phenomena that we observe, from macro-concepts such as consciousness to discrete phenomena such as 'number sense'. And while we can describe emergent behaviours, such as the nature of a conversation between two people, it is impossible for us to write down all the neural activities that go on during the conversation. Or as Ian Stewart and Jack Cohen succinctly put it: 'If our brains were simple enough for us to understand them, we'd be so simple that we couldn't.'[58]

In the absence of direct insights, teachers must rely on inferences and working models for affecting learning. We use metaphors to talk about our children's minds – schema, attentiveness, understanding, forgetting. For the teacher facing a class, it is unrealistic to *ever* ascertain fully what prior knowledge they are building upon for that lesson. It is unrealistic to precisely measure what sort of connected knowledge and understanding has been built once the lesson has ended. And even if it superficially appears that something has been learned during a lesson, it is difficult to predict what this means for longer term changes in knowledge and understanding in each child's mind.

Emergent behaviours of children – such as answering questions correctly – may appear similar on the surface, however we do not know whether the neural activities are similar or not, either between individuals or between one instance of a child's response and another. Therefore, we cannot be sure that we are all on the same well-defined path to learning. We are all on an intellectual journey, but we do not know what it is.

Our inability to read minds and our limited understanding of how to consistently change them means that even for a single, isolated child, learning cannot be consistently predicted, measured or produced. Despite all the advances in neuroscience, there is little prospect of teachers ever being able to teach with a complete understanding of what their class knew before or learned during the lesson.

The class is a mere abstraction

Diagnosing the learning needs of an individual child in a tutoring situation is difficult, and the studies of overconfidence and misdiagnosis by medical doctors in one-on-one situations suggest we would be naïve to assume that educational tutors can do this perfectly.[59] Teachers in schools face an even greater challenge because they do not teach individual children; they teach a class. We task them with progressing a class from knowledge point A to knowledge point B in a fixed period – the lesson. This mass schooling act of changing 30 different minds in a class in a consistent manner over the period of a lesson is the essential feature that brings structure, order, scalability and efficiency to our education system. The challenge of doing so is not 30 times more complicated than teaching an individual child. It is infinitely more complex, necessarily involving guesswork and compromise. There is no correct way to teach any particular 'class' any particular new concept, for the class is a mere abstraction that does not, in fact, exist.

The 'You Should Know This' moment occurs due to a failure to appreciate and predict which children will have successfully learned something in the past and which will not have. They are inevitable because of the huge diversity within a class in what students happen to know at any point in time, and in their capability to learn and take on new ideas within the confines of the lesson. The reasons for this diversity across students in a class are complex and so defy concise explanation. Some 'will not know it' because they missed the lesson where it was taught entirely. Others 'will not know it' because they were inattentive as the point was being made during the prior lesson. Others may have listened attentively but not understood and assimilated the new idea, perhaps because they lacked the prerequisite knowledge to do so. Others may have felt they understood it at the time, yet now have no recollection of exactly what the idea was.

Amplifying gaps

Almost every discipline within the social sciences has a set of theories that contribute to explaining why children differ so much in their capabilities to learn. By looking at a child through their own theoretical lens, each disciplinary tradition simplifies this variation down to causal dynamics that are distinctive in both the level at which they analyse the problem and the phenomena they choose to focus on. Like Russian nesting dolls, as each disciplinary perspective is unpacked, it merely reveals another of the seemingly endless series of theoretical descriptions of the world. Each doll, or discipline, contains some degree of 'truth' and utility, but none can paint a complete picture.

Take, for example, the disciplines of economics and sociology. While they care little for each other's approaches, they share the perspective that the root cause of differences in attainment are social, economic and cultural deficits in home life or in quality of schooling. This points to a solution in the form of extra 'educational inputs', such as extra funding to educate children from low-income households. They use attainment gaps between students from higher and lower income households to 'prove' their causal story is correct, while overlooking the considerable variation in educational success between siblings who live together that cannot be explained by their theories.[60]

Psychological traditions, by contrast, start with the individual and their cognitive traits. Geneticists will use comparisons of identical and non-identical twins to show how a large proportion of the population variation in attainment (anywhere from 40% to 80%) seems to be attributable to genetic, rather than environmental, factors.[61] However, this suggested heritability of both intelligence and attainment tells us nothing about why it is so. Cognitive psychologists will try to unpeel what this variation in 'intelligence' is attributable to, perhaps emphasising the variation in children's executive function such as their working memory or attentiveness. Since improving executive function is generally agreed to be beyond the scope of what schools can do, some view these perspectives as defeatist, providing no clear answer to how we can ensure all children can progress from Knowledge Point A to Knowledge Point B together within the course of a lesson. However, the more optimistic psychologists give advice about how we can optimise teaching to support those with poorer executive function.

Each of these traditions ignore the dynamics of the classroom, so to unpeel these we must turn to social psychologists who explore the behavioural origins of attitudes to learning, motivation and self-image. Learning does not take place unless we persuade children to attend to the content of the lesson. Thus, studying how we can improve students' likelihood of engaging with learning, both at home and at school, is as important as understanding their capacity to do so. Social psychologists' analysis of the problem lends itself to solutions such as reward and behaviour management policies, growth mindset interventions, studies of peer group influences and so on.

Finally, there are the educationalists. Education is not really a discipline as such, but what unites educationalists is a belief that schooling matters so the location of, and solution to, inequalities in attainment must lie with them. Educationalists with an interest in curriculum theory will emphasise failures to carefully map out and arrange the way in which new ideas and topics are taught to ensure that schema are developed effectively. Those interested in pedagogy will carve a career exploring inequalities that arise from how feedback is given, or how to facilitate effective learning activities, or the arrangement of seating in a class. Others take a managerialist line that we can reduce the variation in the quality of teaching across classrooms through instruments such as audits, pay incentives and league tables.

All disciplines can agree that students who sit in the same lessons do not make equal learning gains; they simply disagree on which types of causal explanations are most productive to focus on. It is not possible to say which cause is the most significant, since attributing proportionate causality is impossible in a complex system where biological and environmental causes interact to create positive feedback loops.[62] Tiny gaps in one attribute are amplified to create large end-point differences in attainment.

To understand these positive feedback loops, let us tell the story of Abby, Brian, Caspar, Diana and the sandcastle building tournament. In each round of this tournament, the children must perfectly copy a picture of a sandcastle using their own bucket and the sand around them. The sandcastle instructions for each round build directly on the sandcastle structure that was completed in the round before.

Round one begins and they start building their castles. Diana is quickly in trouble since she has never built one before so at first does not appreciate the importance of finding wet sand on the beach. By the time she picks up how to do this the round is finished. In round two Diana is having to build her additional sand structures on top of a shaky foundation. Should she go back and fix it first or just plough on? Either way, it is hard to see how she will catch up, despite having now mastered how to build sandcastles. Small differences in prior knowledge on which to build new ideas can often create large differences in attainment further down the road, especially in subjects where foundations are critical.

Brian has built sandcastles before so has no difficulty getting started, but he quickly sees that his bucket is less effective than Abby's. It is an awkward shape making it slightly slower to produce each little sand mound. Before long, this tiny difference in the shape of his bucket is producing large differences in the look of his sandcastle because he fails to fully complete each round as the competition progresses. Children sitting together in class often have these tiny differences in working memory or other aspects of executive function, but if each round of lessons moves on regardless of whether they feel secure in the last one, it is easy to see how these tiny differences compound into large attainment gaps.

Caspar is younger than the others and at first does not really appreciate that this isn't a bit of fun – it is a very serious competition that he needs to work hard at. It certainly does not feel like fun anymore at the end of the first round, when Abby clearly has a better sandcastle. Caspar decides to try to take round two more seriously, but by then frustration starts to kick in as he realises he cannot catch up. Motivation is an important determinant of how much effort we put into learning, but success in learning is also an important determinant of motivation.[63] Given this, is it any surprise that those students with initial curiosity about something who engage and experience success early on tend to like continuing to learn it the most?

Managing small differences in children's prior learning, cognitive function or interests in learning within the classroom *would* be possible, were the game to start afresh each lesson. Imagine there were few dependencies between what is learned in one lesson and what is learned in the next. This would allow the class to arrive together at the start of a lesson fully able to engage in it. And while some might progress faster during the class thanks to differences in motivation or executive function, this would have no impact on what happens during the next class. The challenge of the classroom arises because small differences in knowledge, effort or cognition are destined to become amplified through positive feedback loops.[64]

A lesson in myth and reality

These two fundamental problems in schooling – the invisibility of learning and the lock-step problem of meeting the needs of diverse children – make the idea of the 'lesson' as the unit of progression a complete fantasy, both for the teacher and each student. The teacher cannot start the lesson at a point that suits the class's prior knowledge because there is no collective starting point.

Teachers are necessarily forced to deal in these simplified stories of the classroom. The idea that a class can and should know specific things provides teachers with a practical working model by which to plan and teach. However, interpreting this as a direct representation of how a class can and should be can lead to unrealistic expectations of ordered and homogenous learning outcomes.

The 'You' in the 'You Should Know This' moment captures the necessity and limitations of the model a teacher uses when teaching a class. 'You' is a reification of the class, turning the abstract conception of 'class' into an objective being. Teachers often speak of what they have taught their classes, what their class has learned, how well-motivated their class is and so forth. This is reflected in the way that teachers personify a class as 'difficult' or 'great to teach'. However, who is the teacher referring to? The best they can do is hold in their heads some approximation of their class, encapsulated perhaps as a fictional child on which decisions are made.

Going further, the two fundamental problems mean that the classroom and progress made within it cannot be fully comprehended by a teacher. There is unknowledge – areas where it is not possible for the teacher to know the state of the classroom. This was beautifully illustrated in the late Graham Nuthall's book *The Hidden Lives of Learners* (2007), which documented the experiences, conversations and work of pupils across a series of lessons, highlighting important features and significant variation in their individual classroom experiences. His insights puncture any ideas one might have about the classroom being a tight run ship where all students made predictable progress under their teacher's expert instruction.[65]

Classrooms exude complexity – poorly understood and emergent states at any point in time. Classes develop a culture and attitudes to learning that cannot be understood in terms of the individual children's dispositions. Learning in a classroom is a social act mediated by the relationships that students have with their peers as well as their teacher. These relationships and the rules governing them influence all students, but not in the same way. One's place in the social strata, for example, may permit or forbid certain behaviours, while others experience the inverse. There are differences in how willing students are to ask their peers, or the teacher, when they do not understand or are confused. Students are often reluctant to reveal high levels of understanding as much as they are their ignorance. Individual student ideas about classroom behaviours combine to produce new classroom norms, that in turn shape future classroom behaviours that might have been quite different given small differences in starting points or events. This is the reason teachers say to one another: 'Oh, they aren't like that for me.' Nuthall's work, which used microphones to record individual student talk, helps highlight the diversity of experiences students have within the complex and unstable social context of a classroom. This applies even to topic-focused talk between students (of course Nuthall's microphones picked up numerous interactions entirely unrelated to learning). Students who know what to do, or how to answer certain questions, become gatekeepers of that knowledge. Their less knowledgeable peers can find it hard to get this information out of them and may risk humiliation when doing so. Even in the case of written work, Nuthall concluded that class dynamics emerge whereby most students seek to work at a rate that avoids the teacher's notice. Working too slowly, or too quickly, invites attention and is to be avoided wherever possible. The social norms of the class are emergent: they are simultaneously determined by individual productivity *and,* in turn, determine individual productivity.

Problems without solutions

We call the invisibility of learning and the need for lock-step progression of diverse children the fundamental problems in schooling because we view them as problems to be managed, rather than fixed. Technologists regularly claim that we will soon be able to fix the invisibility of learning, using assessments and technology to provide the teacher with a clear understanding of whether each student in a class knows any given idea. We describe one manifestation of this data movement in chapter 5. While progress can and will be made to improve assessment of learning, we are sceptical that this area of teacher's unknowledge will ever be remediated, for unless we fully understand knowledge structures in the brain we will not know what prior knowledge our tests need to uncover.

But suppose for a moment we do enable the teacher to fully view the prior knowledge of students, thus partially fixing the first fundamental problem in schooling, what should the teacher do next? Knowledge of the vast variation in prior knowledge may simply introduce a quandary where blissful ignorance once existed. In research using meticulously designed pre- and post-teaching tests, Nuthall found that pupils knew, on average, 50% of what teachers were about to teach them. The difficulty was that, even on learning this information, the teacher was able to do nothing with it. For not only did some students have more prior knowledge, and some less, each student knew a different set of pieces of prior information. So, there was no easy shortcut to cutting material from the lesson to avoid repetition or way to add additional teaching to top up deficiencies across the class. Pupils recognise this quandary – it is why they quickly learn to keep quiet about the fact that 'they already know this' because saying so neither endears them to the teachers, nor enables the teachers to adjust their instruction.

Some argue we can compensate for deficient prior vocabulary or differences in cultural capital through teaching; these are simply re-encapsulations of the same arguments across different subject disciplines.[66] If deficiencies in background knowledge, skill levels, vocabulary or cultural experiences are both variable in size and uniquely different in each child, then there is no mass schooling intervention that can efficiently compensate. This is not to say that we cannot and should not ever plug gaps in prior learning, but that we need to do it based on a more nuanced understanding of the extent to which the prior learning is an essential prerequisite for moving forward in the curriculum or not.[67]

Asking the impossible

Individual lessons, in which students of similar biological age are taught a specific aspect of the curriculum, are the bricks with which we seek to construct ambitious educational edifices. Sweeping educational reforms intended to make a mark upon the social world are premised upon teachers' capacity to teach specific ideas, to specific classes, within a specific timeframe. Lessons are a compelling basis for building education since children can arrive in a class having experienced the same set of lessons in the past and so having the same set of building blocks in place on which to add the next brick. We have forgotten, if we ever knew, that the 'class' and 'progress through a curriculum' are mere abstractions. The lesson as we imagine it is not a fundamental building block; it is a long-since reified procedural regularity.

Unless students all join their classes with identical abilities, background knowledge, motivation and interests, it is unavoidable that there will be variations in what they learn in lessons. Time and content pressures and variation in ability and background knowledge will push teachers to, consciously or subconsciously, make compromises. When made consciously this necessitates acknowledging that they will likely benefit some in their care more than others. At other times, perhaps decisions are rationalised with a narrative that rewrites them as inevitable or places culpability elsewhere: 'You Should Know This'.

In the 'You Should Know This' moment, a teacher's unknowledge is compounded by the demands that the lock-step model of schooling places upon them and their students. The 'You Should Know This' moment is frustrating for the students, but it is equally unpleasant for the teacher who is given the impossible task of ensuring that a diverse set of children all learn the same curriculum within a fixed time schedule. The US sociologist Seymour B. Sarason remarked that he had 'never met a teacher who was not aware of and disturbed by the fact that he or she had not the time to give to some children in the class the kind of help they needed – and the need for help, it should be emphasised, is frequently not due to any basic intellectual defect'. He went on to say that asking the impossible of teachers means 'that they have no difficulty finding occasions that prove their inadequacy'.[68]

And yet we *must* organise schooling around these building blocks of lessons and orderly curriculum progress, however fictional they are, because the alternatives are too complex to contemplate and implement. It is the product of the compromise between the needs of the individual and those of the many that mass schooling necessitates. At its core lie the tensions and contradictions built into the teacher's task of inducing specific learning (which is challenging enough in itself) in a group of students simultaneously.

You Should Know This. While students perceive blame when they hear this phrase uttered by teachers, perhaps this is not how it is meant. Perhaps it is simply uttered as a self-evident statement of how things ought to be, were it not for the complexity of the task. If we can come to terms with the fundamental problems of schooling and understand teaching as the art of imperfection and compromise, we might stand a better chance of ensuring more students do 'know this'.

Complex advice

Teaching is destined to be difficult as the teacher faces intractable dilemmas. However, by understanding these fundamental problems teachers can appreciate the diversity of the classroom and perhaps come to terms with the imperfection of their craft.

To learn to live with classroom diversity we suggest the following:

1. When you find yourself personifying a class, think about the children who do not fit this description and remember that the emergent behaviours of a group do not necessarily reflect a common trait of those in the group.
2. Do not assume that because a class has been taught something they should all know it.
3. Diversity is amplified over time. Remember that there is no simple causal reason for educational gaps or any catch-all solutions. It is not within the power of one teacher, or one school, to overcome the divergence of human experience.
4. Draw on multiple disciplines to make sense of what you see and avoid relying on one disciplinary field.
5. We cannot hope to understand the complexity of the brain, so instead we use metaphors for learning – schema, learning gaps, lost learning, attentiveness, progress, attainment, special needs. We should continually question the usefulness of these conceptions and whether they serve the purpose of improving children's learning.

Reflective questions

- If you are a teacher, think of a class you teach. How would you describe them? What is your reference point for how you personify the class?
- What disciplinary perspectives are invoked most frequently in your experience to either explain what is happening or justify what should happen in a school? Who invokes these disciplines and what may be their reason for doing so?
- What causal explanations for learning gaps resonate with you the most? What makes these explanations attractive?
- Do you recognise the predicaments that the children in the sandcastle story find themselves in?
- How do schools and teachers attempt to overcome the problem of the invisibility of learning? To what extent have they been successful?
- What practical strategies do teachers use to attempt to overcome the lock-step problem?

CHAPTER 4 – FORGOTTEN LESSONS

> *The central challenge for us is how we resolve the tensions between a universal system and personal needs, between excellence and equity ... [Personalisation] means something very simple for me; it means an education system tailored to the needs, interests and aptitudes of every single pupil.*
>
> David Miliband, speaking in 2004[69]

In the early 2000s, a new policy emerged in the UK out of the rising tide of individualism in the wider society. The personalised learning agenda felt fresh, exciting and important. It promised to solve the fundamental problem of how to educate children with diverse prior knowledge and aptitudes, progressing at varying paces towards different destinations, in our one-size-fits-all classrooms. Personalised learning seemed novel and modern. As technology was reshaping societal and economic structures, so teachers must respond by preparing children for this rapidly changing and uncertain future. (You may remember the viral video *Shift Happens*,[70] which was shown in assemblies up and down the country.) The sentiment and ideology of a movement committed to meeting the unique needs of every child was hard to argue against. It appealed to the imagined range of actions of teachers: they could be saviours of the disadvantaged, social reformers and child-centred public servants.

There is no better encapsulation of the imagined success that personalisation could yield than the story of a young person called James, as recounted in a 2004 government publication.[71] James, born of a heroin addict, growing up in an area of high unemployment and deprivation, resistant to the efforts of school to make him attend, is liberated from his circumstances through a 'personal programme' that James himself co-designed, which enabled him to access the services he needed. James was 'allowed to do the activities he liked – sports and cooking' and eventually starts to re-engage in school with the help of a 'learning manager' whose job 'was to work with James and find out what he wanted to do'. James's life, we are told, is 'transformed'.

The paper highlights the core ingredients of personalised learning. First, that the school is more 'customer focused' by considering student experience and giving them greater voice in the choices available. Second, that the student can act as the co-designer of services, so feeling more committed than they would as passive consumers of education. Third, that the 'script' of educational service provision, which has not changed for decades, is rewritten to produce transformative outcomes. These ingredients echoed the New Labour government public service reform programmes that reimagined the state as a 'strategic trader',[72] *steering* activity through targets and choice.

Little did they know that the movement teachers were encouraged to subscribe to was as old as the schooling system itself. For children have always arrived in the classroom with different prior knowledge, skills and capabilities to take on new ideas. And so, educators have always wrestled with their desire or need to instruct collectively while simultaneously wanting to deliver what each child needs. What felt like a once-and-for-all-time solution to this fundamental problem turned out to be simply the latest failed solution to a dilemma that has plagued education for as long as schools have opened their doors.

In the last chapter, we introduced the fantastical idea of 'the lesson', an imaginary collective experience whereby a class are together led by an expert teacher and moved from one point in the curriculum to another. The organisation of schooling around these collective lessons creates the second fundamental problem of schooling – the lock-step problem. The idea of 'the lesson' persists as an imperfect solution to the complexity of meeting the needs of diverse children and has many advantages beyond its simple organising convenience and efficiency. It allows a mass of children access to an expert teacher that was once the preserve of the rich, and it creates a sense of community and equity, of a generation of children on a journey together.

But while it seems intrinsic to modern schooling, the lesson has not always been the linchpin of mass schooling. Indeed, to arrive in schools it came up against powerful alternative methods of organisation. To see these, let us travel back about 200 years to the early decades of the 19th century, where a new technology was struggling to take hold in American schoolrooms.

The delayed success of the chalkboard

The chalkboard (or blackboard as it also became known in England) promised to become the educational innovation of a new century. Upon observing this new tool in the hands of a skilled instructor, commentators waxed lyrical about its transformative potential for engaging students and creating dynamic lessons.[73] Popular in military academies, where whole-class instruction was the favoured pedagogy, the marks made by chalk against the blackboard provided structure and weight to the explanatory words of the instructor, taking students away from their individual study and bringing pace and energy to the learning process. Educational reformers in the US began pushing for blackboards to be included as standard in the new 'common schools' being constructed across the country.[74] However, this powerful technology did not live up to its early promise. In schoolrooms, blackboards would sit untouched by teachers as students continued to study individually from texts. An 1839 report noted, 'Blackboards are not uncommon, but are little resorted to by the teacher', while a further report in 1842 claims one teacher observed 'knows almost as little about how to use it as his pupils'.[75] This may be no surprise to those of us who taught in schools during the rise and fall of the interactive whiteboards in the early 21st century.

To understand why the chalk and board innovation failed to take hold in American schoolrooms, some context is necessary. Public education was in its infancy in the early 19th century. Mass schooling was a response both to the need to ensure that those recently endowed with democratic voting rights could exercise this power wisely, and to the call for a more educated workforce to further the economic interests of nations as international trade increased. One of the early advocates was Joseph Lancaster, an English born educational reformer and inventor of the monitorial system.[76] Lancaster was influential in England by launching the Lancastrian schooling model, which was built around appointing 'monitors' (older/abler students) to tutor younger students – what might today be called peer mentoring, although the method was more structured than modern peer-to-peer programmes tend to be. When Lancaster emigrated to the United States, he found his ideas had much support and so the monitorial system spread rapidly, first across the US, then into other countries.

Lancaster's system was predicated on the understanding that children each possessed different knowledge and skills when they started school, therefore they would need to begin their study from their personal starting point and work at their own pace. The core disciplines of reading, writing and mathematics were broken down into sequences and pupils were placed at the appropriate point in the learning progression for each. Study was structured through texts, and more competent pupils were appointed to 'monitor' the learning of their peers, equipped with scripted lessons, and told to move them on when they had achieved mastery of the content.

What made the monitorial system so attractive was its scalability. Prior to the move towards mass education, children from affluent backgrounds would receive one-to-one tuition while those from humbler origins would take an apprenticeship and receive individualised instruction from a tradesman. The challenge of universal education was how to give a much larger population of children access to the expansive academic knowledge previously only accessible to the privately tutored. Lancaster's system provided a solution to this problem by creating an untrained army of monitors, under the supervision of the teacher, who would outsource instruction via carefully designed programmes to a group of able students. To increase efficiency further, pupils at a similar point along their learning programme were grouped so that one monitor could oversee the study of more than one pupil.

Given the popularity and economic necessity of the monitorial system, it is no surprise that a new technology that expected the teacher to instruct a whole class of pupils in the same material was of absolutely no use at all. The chalkboards were a novelty that no doubt provided amusement for the children who would dare to draw upon it when the teacher's back was turned, but as an instructional tool they arrived decades too soon for many educational institutions. Personalised learning, not whole-class instruction, was the orthodoxy of the day; the blackboard just did not make sense to teachers given their conception of what they were being expected to do.

Of course, all of this changed, and the blackboard eventually became a well-used, standard piece of teaching equipment, replaced only by the board marker and wipeable whiteboards that entered schools in the late 20th century. The blackboard became useful when the model of schooling changed again. Lancaster himself was a part of the change that would eventually mean the monitorial system's fall from favour. He noticed that grouping of students by competency stigmatised older, less advanced pupils who found themselves tutored with much younger children.

We can imagine the 'depressed' and 'discouraged' senior boys, not so very different from those we see in lower sets in today's schools, who became disenfranchised with schooling, and who were likely a disruptive influence on their younger peers. Lancaster wrote of a 'boy, named Harvey, [who] was once allured into bad company, in whose society, his lively, playful mind found more pleasure than in school'.[77] Harvey's father took a firm disciplinary approach to his correction, while his teacher attempted to gently coerce him into studying, neither of which was successful. Many innovations emerged to maintain the cooperation of those like Harvey – competitions, incentives, common kindness – which foreshadow the efforts of modern educators who have become adept, but little more successful, at overcoming a problem of our own making. The educational deviant persona emerged: the label 'retarded student' was coined and applied (although the language changes) to generations of children ever since, most recently in the rhetoric about 'stuck' pupils that foreshadowed the intervention culture of the 2010s.[78]

Out of this self-imposed dilemma emerged age-related, mixed-ability groupings. These more flexible grouping systems suited the growing number and scale of urban schools. Unlike rural schools who dealt with small numbers of pupils, known well by their teachers who lived in the community, urban schools faced a greater number and diversity of intake. Economies of scale were required, which necessitated larger groupings and enabled teacher specialisation (a maths teacher, a history expert, a literary specialist). Within these larger schools, children of similar age were increasingly expected to learn the same content and progress at the same pace: in 'lock-step' fashion. In this emerging educational landscape, driven by economic necessity and social change, the blackboard found its place as the technology of choice for 'chalk and talk' pedagogues.

A hundred years after the peak of Lancaster's schooling system, the American educator Ellwood Patterson Cubberley wrote in a state of the fundamental principles of education that precisely 70.4% of students should be progressing in line with age-related expectations, while the remainder would be 'lagging' or 'accelerating'.[79] A further century later, and these expectations are strangely born out in our GCSE pass rates, whereby approximately 70% meet our expectations for what a good outcome looks like, while a cohort of Harveys (and they are disproportionately boys) are left behind. If Harvey had been born 200 years later, perhaps he would have been given a personal mentor, or be part of an intervention programme due to his failure to keep on the flight path.

Personalising lock-step schooling

The story of the initial failure, then success, of the chalkboard illustrates two fundamentally opposing solutions to the problem of how to educate individuals through a mass schooling system. On the one hand, we have an attempt to personalise schooling such that each child progresses from their own starting point and at their own pace. On the other, we have lock-step pedagogy whereby students of similar age are exposed to the curriculum at a pace determined by the teacher.

The tension between these two approaches is summed up by the sociologist Seymour B. Sarason in his critique of the dominant lock-step model:

> A graded school system, taking a new crop of children every year at five to six years of age, moving them through their studies in 'lock-step' fashion 'til graduation, makes an assumption about the equality, motivation, and performance for children of similar age that the reality of individual differences rudely challenges.[80]

The failure of lock-step schooling is in its denial of individual differences in prior knowledge and cognitive capabilities, although the model is practicable and reasonably effective for many. On the other hand, while personalised approaches attempt to cater for difference, they do so with a level of complexity that prevents their application at scale. Both solutions are imperfect, each giving rise to further, ultimately irresolvable problems as they are born from a tension that lies at the heart of any system of mass schooling. In chapter 3, we described how the teacher experiences this tension within their classroom in the form of the words 'You Should Know This'.

We face a fundamental irresolvable dilemma: how do we reconcile the need to educate large numbers of children in a defined body of knowledge, and finite timescale, while acknowledging the different starting points and pace at which they can acquire this knowledge? Where children are diverse, we can meet the desires of collectivity – of educating a group with an expert teacher – or we can meet the needs of the individual child, taking them precisely from the cusp of what they know, on a journey at a pace and in a direction that suits them best. Collectivism or individualism; never at once.

This dichotomy gives rise to perpetual ideological pendulum swings in education, as we try to disrupt the efficient yet imperfect solution of the lesson to meet the needs of the individual child. The principles of the monitorial system of schooling have not been retired in favour of the lock-step model; rather they re-emerge in disguised forms.

Sometimes we try to disrupt 'the lesson' in subtle ways, such as asking teachers to 'differentiate' their instruction and resources to attend to different levels of prior knowledge within a single class. Differentiation is an example of a *mandatory miracle,* a poorly specified instruction to teachers that they should perform tasks that solve a fundamental problem of schooling. There are so many definitional inconsistencies that it is difficult to know what is being enacted in the name of differentiation, so researchers have struggled to even document its use, let alone analyse its effectiveness as an instructional approach.[81] It can be anything from presuming that some students will complete more of a worksheet than others, through to teaching groups within a class entirely separately, through to letting students teach themselves and progress at a pace that suits them through booklets or computer programmes. (Some readers may remember the School Mathematics Project (SMP) mathematics booklets of the 1980s, which allowed mixed-ability maths 'teaching' by having children learn with very little collective instruction at all.)

The presumption is often that differentiation is good for students, albeit burdensome for teachers, but this presupposes that prior knowledge and learning capabilities of individual students are well-understood by teachers – a violation of our first fundamental problem of schooling.[82] This may be one of the many reasons why studies of differentiated instruction programmes, even ones with extensive training and coaching in place, often find they cannot evaluate differentiation because it simply isn't being done.[83] Usually these criticisms of differentiation are simply dismissed by its advocates on the basis that differentiation is 'poorly understood'.[84] Well, of course it is – all miracles are.

Every so often, the pendulum swings a little further away from lock-step schooling towards approaches that are more closely inspired by the monitorial system. The 'mastery' movement, popular in maths, is an example of disrupting the idea that there is a Year 3 curriculum through the mantra 'Stage not Age'. Students should start each lesson where they are and finish each lesson where they are able to get to.[85] We have heard proponents of this approach explain that some children need to spend more time learning fractions, others learning algebra. This may be, but how can they do this while sitting in the same class, unless we arrange additional catch-up and practice lessons outside hours (as other countries do)? More importantly, the reality is that the same children are likely to find both fractions and algebra hard, so giving each child adequate time to 'master' each new idea will quickly create divergence in speed of progression along the curriculum. Before long, 14-year-olds will find themselves in classrooms with seven-year-olds, and all the problems of the monitorial system will reveal themselves again.

Lock-step schooling is the flawed system that we are willing to live with, despite the impossibility of what it asks of us. Teachers will criticise the consequences of the system: the requirement to cover material regardless of the needs of the individual child, how certain children are necessarily left by the wayside, the enormous complexity of what teachers are asked to do with their 30 students. However, few teachers ever question the lock-step schooling model that creates their problems in the first place.[86] Even when older students are grouped into sets by prior attainment, we would prefer not to acknowledge that it becomes increasingly difficult for children to move across attainment sets as the content and pace of the curriculum diverges. The myth of the collective experience of the universal lock-step curriculum is a powerful one.

The mystery of the Personalised Learning agenda

The Personalised Learning agenda of the early 2000s denied irresolvable problems and unpalatable trade-offs as much as every other solution that had come before it over the centuries. It suited a New Labour government committed to using school autonomy and incentives to improve educational performance. Personalisation simplified complex problems by simply empowering schools to deliver large-scale transformation and improvement in the system. They were asked to perform miracles, albeit poorly specified ones. The approaches they were asked to consider included: greater flexibility in timetabling; grouping and curriculum, opening education to the wider community; emphasising greater collaboration between students, teachers and parents; using technology to enhance learning; and using data to intervene at the point when students begin to fall behind.[87]

These new activities, by their very nature, injected greater complexity into schools, with increased interdependencies of previously siloed parts of the school, decision making individualised to students rather than year groups and new layers of monitoring and accountability to track the progress of pupils to facilitate individualised decision making. It was accompanied by a cacophony of other policy initiatives, all representing a swing away from collectivism and towards individualism: Personal, Learning and Thinking Skills (PeLTS), diplomas, Every Child Matters, Assessment for Learning, virtual learning platforms, extended services, multiple intelligences, Gifted and Talented schemes, interventions, Social and Emotional Aspects of Learning (SEAL), learning styles, learning pathways, and student voice. As Basil Bernstein observes, 'Every time a discourse moves, there is space for ideology to play.'[88] Personalisation was the most playful of policy initiatives at the start of this century.

Teachers were told that personalisation was not optional – it was a matter of moral purpose and social justice.[89] Nobody involved in education could deny that meeting the needs of every individual child is an excellent idea, but what does this mean policymakers, headteachers and classroom teachers should actually do? For policy officials, personalisation was little more than a narrative, a social manifesto rather than a policy instrument. Sociologists Maguire, Ball and Braun characterise personalisation as a 'polyphonic, multiple policy agenda' as it is so broad in calling for transformation of many aspects of school business: curriculum choice, teaching, guidance and school organisation.[90] However, this broadness in its appeal was also its weakness, as it could mean almost anything to anyone; its boundaries were very ill-defined. It was both easy to ignore or to claim that it was already 'being done'.

When asked, teachers and school leaders would claim to be delivering on the personalised learning agenda already due to their implementation of differentiation, inclusion, careers guidance, parental involvement, curriculum choice, specials needs provision and gifted and talented programmes.[91] This post hoc rationalisation of policy implementation meant schools could *look* like they had responded to policy, while continuing to pursue the practices they had already chosen because they were right for their context. When policies are nothing more than wishful thinking – a hint to schools as to what they should believe and pursue without clear instruction or sufficient tools – they dissipate and fail to result in meaningful change. Politicians eager to make their mark, and with an aversion to meddling directly with the workings of society, create a plethora of policies directed towards the school as the engine for societal change, rather than at the teacher who holds the power to help a child learn. Misdirection, ambiguity and overload create a potent mix of transient change and avoidance.

An unfolding story

As enthusiasm for personalisation waned, the problem it was trying to solve did not go away. Young people, like James in the story at the start of the chapter, continued to fall behind at school, become disenchanted with education and be 'failed' by the system. Personalised Learning had not delivered on its promise to radically transform schools, but the search for a solution would continue.

Arguably, many (perhaps all) of the problems we grapple with in education are of our own making and reoccur in different forms over time. The two fundamental problems of schooling can never be solved. The desire and/or necessity (according to how you look at it) to create a system of education where every child can succeed over a fixed period of time sets up irresolvable dilemmas, which in turn create persistent problems that emerge and re-emerge again and again. Within each new solution sits a particular conceptualisation of the problem, one that is shaped by the unintended consequences of the previous solution. For example, the desire to personalise learning revealed a deficiency in teachers' knowledge about where students were in their learning, which invited a solution that claimed to address this deficiency (the 'data' solution that we will explore in the next chapter). In attempting to solve the persistent problems in education, we push them underground for a while, but they arise in new forms, bearing the hallmarks of our previous attempts to solve them. We term these phenomena 'metamorphic problems' because they constantly change in form, and yet are always hiding somewhere. These problems are endemic in our schooling system, are enduring and irresolvable and are one of the reasons we keep trying (and often failing) to improve schools.

As we tell the story of Personalised Learning, we do so as a narrator who knows the whole narrative, with the benefit of hindsight and omniscience. To those living the events as they unfold, this privileged position is not attainable. We do not know how the story will unfold and where it will end. In the moment, what is happening often feels normal and right – it is just how it is. Stepping outside of one's place in time requires exceptional insight and objectivity.

What might we learn from these stories that will make us act more wisely in the present? Perhaps we should start by noting that reforms that seem reasonable at the time will probably, with hindsight, appear quaint, odd or even absurd. The objectives we pursue, the things we spend time trying to change, the way we direct resources and energy, depend upon the prevailing orthodoxy of the time. Proponent or not, the prevailing orthodoxy in education is always one we must be subject to. Adopting a cautious scepticism of what might present itself as an obvious solution or appealing intervention may help us guard against misadventure.

We might also observe that the problems we strive to overcome are not new. They arise from irresolvable dilemmas, built into the education system, that continually re-emerge in new forms, bearing the hallmarks of our previous imperfect attempts to solve them. It is human nature to want to fix the problems in schooling, but to do so means denying complexity and the existence of the fundamental problems in schooling. Policymakers will always generate new policy ideas that usually deny complexity and fundamental problems. Occasionally, rather than denying the fundamental problems, they will acknowledge them and claim they can be fixed. Either way, we should be sceptical.

The moral arguments for personalisation are admirable but are undeliverable given the need to deliver an efficient model of education at scale. Of course, each generation will go on its own quest to resolve these tensions, and each will hope for the miracles the system so desperately needs. But perhaps if we simply acknowledge there are constraints and trade-offs, that there are values implicit in the trade-off we choose and that the right trade-offs will vary by school, by subject, by cultural setting, then we may find more peace of mind when confronted with our inevitable 'failures', and so have the psychological strength to carry on.

Complex advice

Personalising the learning experience for every child is a tempting, but unforgiving task. By accepting the constraints of mass schooling we may find pragmatic ways to help individuals find success and overcome adversity.

To avoid being overwhelmed by the urge to personalise, we would suggest:

1. Look for technologies that genuinely achieve personalised instruction in a way that a teacher cannot achieve alone.
2. Learn to recognise the persistent problems of schooling as they emerge in new forms. Notice how they manifest, taking on the characteristics of the context in which they are observed.
3. When new policies arise, question what problem they are intended to solve. Does the policy promise to solve the irresolvable?
4. Recognise the trade-offs that come with a decision to act. A system with finite resources cannot be all things to all people.
5. Do not berate yourself too harshly for being taken in by past movements, fads and ideological positions. Know that it will happen again.

Reflective questions

- Do you recognise the 'deviant personas' of pupils like James and Harvey? To what extent do you attribute their behaviour to a trait of the child or a consequence of the system?
- What educational technology do teachers use, or get asked or even told to use? Are these attempts to improve whole-class instruction (for example, visualisers) or personalised learning (for example, individualised online assessment tools)?
- If we accept the lock-step problem as a fundamental problem of schooling, what should we reasonably expect teachers to achieve with the children they teach?
- What examples have you witnessed of schools paying 'lip service' to educational policy while continuing to pursue their own agenda? Why does this happen? What makes it possible?
- What persistent problems continually re-emerge in schools? Select one and think about the various forms this problem takes and the range of solutions proposed to 'solve' it. To what extent, and for how long, have these solutions had an effect?

CHAPTER 5 – GREAT BIG SPREADSHEETS

We pass through the present with our eyes blindfolded.
We are permitted merely to sense and guess at what
we are actually experiencing. Only later when the
cloth is untied can we glance at the past and find out
what we have experienced and what meaning it has.

Milan Kundera, *Laughable Loves*[92]

Caught up in a surge of data washing across English schools, it was difficult during the 2010s to step back and observe objectively what was going on. It felt like the flood of data was upon us quite suddenly and there was no time to question its source, or indeed its motivations. But all such movements arise from somewhere: some ideology, intent or attempt to solve an intractable problem. The call to 'personalise' schooling laid the foundations for the subsequent data wave. The desire to know the progress each child is making in their learning – where they are along some imaginary flight path – was, in part, born out of a belief that knowing each child's exact place in their personal educational journey would allow us to respond to their precise needs and ambitions. As personalisation sought to fix the second fundamental problem in schooling (the lock-step problem), it in turn required us to fix the first fundamental problem in schooling – the invisibility of learning.

These fundamental problems continually re-emerge throughout the history of modern education. Ben, as a teacher seeking promotion in 2012, was swept up in the data manifestation of these eternal struggles.

Following a day of interviews, he was called in to see his headteacher. It wasn't good news:

> *Unfortunately, your application for Assistant Headteacher has been unsuccessful. However, we would like to offer you a role as a Raising Standards Leader. It is like being a mini-Ofsted inspector for the school. Your job will be to analyse the data and identify any significant gaps. You then pass your analysis to relevant staff members – Heads of Department, the pastoral team, the Senior Leadership Team. This will help them focus on useful interventions and will keep us all accountable for closing attainment gaps in our school.*

Ben took the job, though he never precisely understood the role or how to make it work. Through attending courses run by professional development companies, he learned that it primarily entailed identifying and closing attainment gaps. This was done by making great big spreadsheets.

The rise of the spreadsheet

Like genetic mutations, new ideas (or new ways of organising existing ideas) are common in education. But only a handful of them replicate rapidly, perhaps subtly changing as they do so, until eventually they become dominant across the system. As one of these successful mutations, the education spreadsheet was not designed, but instead emerged, constantly changing its shape and purpose as it gathered momentum. This momentum took hold because the spreadsheet contained three things: a compelling motive, an appealing method for achieving something and a mechanism for propagation.

The motive to measure pupil learning emerged not only from the needs of the personalisation movement, described in the previous chapter, but also from the decades long march towards greater accountability for quality of schooling through the publishing of school performance tables. In the late 1990s, the new national key stage tests provided the analysts working in Local Education Authorities access to hundreds of thousands of data points on the students in their schools. They saw an opportunity to find out which of their schools was providing a good education through value-added analysis, rather than which simply have affluent intakes. A worthy endeavour. The Department for Education and Skills (DfES) saw the considerable potential value of this data game and contracted the creation and licensing of the National Pupil Database.

If personalisation and accountability were the motives, then the pupil tracking and calculation machines that were built on the National Pupil Database became the method for measuring gaps in learning. Data enthusiasts and new technologies offered a credible and novel high-resolution analysis of what was happening in schools. Commercial organisations sold analysis to schools that made us all acutely aware that not all students learned successfully from teachers. There *were* differences in pupil attainment and progress between and within schools and making these transparent appealed to a range of agents working within the system who, in turn, were able to create new practices that were premised upon the utility of this data. (If we had dwelt on this data more closely we might have been surprised how little schools and teachers explain variation in attainment. Research suggests that schools and teachers only account for about 12% and 17% of all variation in pupil attainment, respectively.[93] That said, variation, however small, there was.) By providing a means of quantifying the problem, the National Pupil Database steered us towards the moral necessity of striving to identify and close these attainment gaps. It appeared obvious that they should do so by analysing their own internal data and intervening where unacceptable gaps were revealed.

A coalition of advocates

Motives and methods for measuring gaps were not quite enough for this new fad to take hold in our fragmented education system where individual schools can make their own choices. For this, we require mechanisms of propagation as key agents gradually start to endorse the use of spreadsheets. The story at the heart of the movement to measure and close attainment gaps gave many people – from policy campaigners through to teachers – an emotionally satisfying role in quantifying and tackling the social problems that educational outcomes reveal. For while classroom teachers and policymakers differ in their level of perspective on the communities they serve, both are united in hoping to make the lives of children – particularly the most disadvantaged – better.

Gradually, a *coalition of advocates* emerged, each with slightly different agendas, but all of them seeing value in enhancing the ways in which our education system produces, analyses and acts upon pupil data. The technology companies were joined by conferences, consultants, school improvement groups and other training providers, including the giant in the field, PiXL. For them, data provided a compelling 'solution' to the riddle of school improvement. They worked to encourage schools to create processes and roles centred on forensically tracking data on the progress of groups.

Data had succeeded in becoming a successful policy mutation, a 'sticky' urban legend or popular theory of the kind that Chip and Dan Heath have studied. For an idea to be 'sticky', easily retained and readily shared, it should be a 'simple, unexpected, concrete, credentialed, emotional story'.[94] The stories emerging around data met these criteria. A *simple* solution. Using novel (if not entirely *unexpected*) means in a *concrete* manner. *Credentialed* by widespread endorsement by experts and leaders and (crucially) offering a hopeful *emotional story* that invites teachers and school leaders to play a vital role in tackling socioeconomic disadvantage.

As a mechanism to propagate ideas through a devolved schooling system, Ofsted's inspection framework is an accelerant more potent than petrol. Once Ofsted joined the coalition of advocates the dominance of data as the primary way of holding schools and teachers to account was complete. Their inspection framework coerced all school leaders to comply with data management, at least on the surface. For example, their 2016 inspection framework implied that all good and outstanding schools would have data showing that pupils made clear progress:

> *Inspectors will consider the progress of pupils currently in the school ... in all year groups, not just those who have taken or are about to take examinations or national tests.*[95]

It even directly stated what the data needed to say for a school to be deemed successful. Pupils needed to be set appropriate targets, which the data movement could invent, against which they made good progress:

> [Inspectors will seek to identify whether] pupils are set challenging goals, given their starting points, and are making good progress towards meeting or exceeding these.[96]

Those less versed in the fragmented or patchwork nature of the English education system started to hear a broadly coherent message coming from a coalition of advocates. However, while an initial glance may give the appearance of a monolithic new feature on the educational horizon, in reality support arose for subtly different reasons and to very different extents.

Many secondary school leaders were early adopters, readily buying tech solutions and seats at conferences. Having been versed in the principles of New Public Management, they readily adopted the idea that generating teacher efficacy and performance targets was a worthwhile pursuit. These leaders were the strongest converts who truly internalised the latest fashion, embracing it wholeheartedly.

Other school leaders gradually came aboard, attracted by the way data promised to tell them what was being learned in their school. For this group, externally conforming was comfortable, even if they suffered from occasional dissonance that data practices did not align with their long-held beliefs about how schooling works.

A third set of school leaders merely complied with the data movement as a strength-in-numbers approach to the accountability culture, where following the herd was a safe leadership strategy.[97] Many of these knew that surface compliance was possible while avoiding most of the more damaging aspects of the movement.

A final set of leaders, usually teaching in small and affluent schools slightly hidden from the accountability system, somehow managed to pretend the data revolution did not exist at all.

Peak data

By 2017, Ben found himself as part of a large and powerful school improvement movement. His new role as a Raising Standards Leader was a sensible appointment in the context of an accountability framework where inspectors would consider in-year assessment data and examine how schools were working to close any gaps that this data revealed. It was better that schools appointed people like Ben to highlight a point of concern than wait for Ofsted to discover it for them during an inspection.

During this period of peak data, most teachers were being asked to submit attainment data to their senior leadership team at least once every half term – data that once sat inside teacher mark books. The lower the Ofsted rating of the school and the more deprived the pupil intake, the greater the 'gaps' on the spreadsheet and so the more frenzied this cycle of data submissions was. Nearly all secondaries were downloading GCSE predictions for their students and using them in a wide variety of ways. Exam results – once the property of the child who sat them – became imbued with meaning and significance that would not have been dreamed of 30 years ago.

For primary teachers, tracking against 'performance statements' rather than concrete tests was common, with four in 10 saying they must track each pupil against more than 50 objectives each year. With 30 pupils in the class, they found themselves making up 1500 annual attainment judgements! Most schools held a subscription to a pupil tracking system that teachers would stare at in the evenings, punching numbers into a screen that got transformed and ingested by those who do not teach – heads, governors, inspectors and parents.[98]

For a while, forensic data analysis offered a compelling solution to the challenges faced by school and system leaders in education. It offered to solve the invisibility of learning problem by revealing both the progress made by individual students and the relative efficacy of individual teachers. In doing so it presented a complicated rather than complex problem for leaders to directly tackle. Data-enriched managerialism had become a culturally established daily part of school leadership – *the* lens (rather than *a* lens) through which the performance of schools, pupils, teachers and leaders would be judged.

Demonstrating progress, precise long-term grade predictions, fine-graded interventions, group-information sheets, boosting the attainment of borderline students, targeting underperformers, flight paths... Through training courses, school policies and the accountability criteria, these terms all gained a *faux solidarity*. They became threads with which we diligently wove the emperor's new clothes. Prevailing orthodoxy maintained that forensic data analysis and interventions were what schools *could* and *should* be doing to ensure that gaps were closed and that all students made progress.

So industrious was this activity that it was easy to mistake all this analysis of gaps, which the system proudly generated, for an explanation of how to fix them, on which the system was more silent.

Doubting data

As time went on, the inadequacies of peak data were increasingly hard to ignore as it became clear that this solution was not working as intended. Many classroom teachers had never bought into the data story, recognising the limitations of data, in particular the misalignment between the numbers on the spreadsheet and the complexity of making sense of what students understand and can do. It was only maths teachers who said they were able to regularly use assessment data to inform teaching and decisions in the classroom. Many teachers said they had access to far more data than they were ever able to make use of. Many teachers believed data collections were too frequent. So did one in five headteachers – a reminder that not everyone who implements a movement also subscribes to it.[99]

Data did little to unmask the invisibility of learning in a manner that was useful for making instructional decisions. In part this resulted from the blunt assessment instruments that constituted the data, often infrequently sat, high-stakes examinations that were rather divorced from the day-to-day classroom experience. But in any case, no assessment would ever work as intended by the policy. For it is necessarily true that learning can only be judged retrospectively and that the learning that happens in the classroom is uncertain, unpredictable and hard to separate from the normal maturation process that takes place regardless of the classroom.[100] Any attempt to measure progress or the quality of teaching through 'assessments' will at best result in an approximation of an approximation.[101] We may capture some residue of the quality of our enacted curriculum, but we cannot be sure that this is evidence of the school's efforts, what value this will be to the child, whether this change is permanent or what else we might have found had we looked for it.

In addition to the data poorly measuring learning needs, students were not, in the main, receiving the 'impactful' forensically targeted interventions that the system was set up to deliver. In part this was due to the second fundamental problem in schooling: the system simply is not set up to attend to the needs of the individual child where they diverge from those of their peers. But it also presumed that leaders and policymakers understand how to fix deficits in learning. And given that the data was a poor proxy for the learning and experiences we wish children to have, by focusing on it narrowly, we risked achieving our targets while damaging our goals. We'd run intervention groups to teach 10-year-olds who have no basic proportionate reasoning how to add up mixed fractions to pass their SATs, for example. In our data pursuit of the superficial, we lost touch somewhat with the complexity of learning.

It seemed like a good idea at the time

The school system is so much more elaborate than the models and explanations that any one of us can articulate. Complex systems are not amenable to being 'solved'. Anybody who wants to, or needs to, believe in widespread system reform is likely to suffer a little from *complexity denial*: a belief that we are more knowledgeable and in control than we actually are. Indeed, we *need* a little complexity denial to protect our sense of self-efficacy. 'Doing data' generally involved complexity denial on an epic scale.

This might have happened because 'doing data' created so much busy activity – reports to be generated, intervention groups to create, pupils' progress to be tracked – that it may have drowned out any signals indicating that systems were not functioning as they should. Furthermore, certainty about the validity of the approach, and clarity around the right actions to take were encouraged, while affording little or no opportunity to voice uncertainty. Ben encountered this as he interviewed colleagues about workload: while they expressed doubts about data in interviews, their daily roles left little space for fully countenancing them and included tasks premised on the validity of data monitoring.[102]

For policymakers and school leaders who are implementing solutions at levels removed from the noise of the classroom, complexity denial is often even greater thanks to the simplified stories that can be told about how things work. Abstracted explanations of schooling that are told in leadership conferences and policy roundtables are usually far clearer and more precise than the day-to-day realities of the classroom. The coalition of advocates tell stories of promised effects that are often ill-defined and disparate. Contrast the neat picture of pupil progress available to a data manager with the stories a class teacher might tell about how their class is progressing. And since classroom teachers are rarely invited to the kind of forums where 'explanations' are formed and utilised, abstraction need never meet reality.

Data was a solution, but it was an ill-fated one, destined to under-deliver on its promises. It offered faux clarity in relation to the fundamental problems of schooling and it denied complexity. Any explanation or solution that is premised on the idea that we can suppress or wish away the fundamental problems of schooling – the invisibility of learning and the lock-step problem – is *necessarily* ill-fated. Ill-fated solutions are not quite the same as miracles that we saw in chapter 4. While personalisation was a mandatory miracle, wishing something were true but providing no instructions as to how to make it possible, 'doing data' contained a very clear set of instructions for action. It is only in its implementation that their redundancy is revealed since the data instructions are missing a sound mechanism by which they will improve a child's knowledge or understanding.

Simplistic explanations of the problem with schooling and the ill-fated solutions that they point towards are perennial features of the educational landscape. Simplicity constituted one of the early appeals of data, but also meant that it would eventually fail on its own terms. The gains that it promised by 'doing data' failed to arrive while the strains and trade-offs involved in propping data up became increasingly visible.

These fads in the form of mandatory miracles and ill-fated solutions do not arise because we are naïve or misguided; rather they are an emergent property of a multi-layered ecosystem with competing objectives and intractable constraints. In the short term at least, adopting complexity-denying solutions may represent a more expedient option for adaptive agents, whether they are working in classroom or policy think tanks. This explanatory monopolisation occurs when a coalition of advocates are, temporarily at least, enthralled by the plausibility of the latest Big Thing and the specific (and necessarily limited) frame of reference within which it sits. What seems like a good idea at the time is only, with hindsight, revealed as merely another ill-fated solution.

The demise of the data

You already know how this story ends. Data scepticism slowly gathered strength by following the same pattern as data optimism before it: at first it is upheld as absurd, then maybe true, and, finally, we knew it all along.[103] Just as the concerted endorsement of various actors led to the rise of data, so a chorus of discord voicing concerns about its limitations and latent effects eventually drove it back down these same steps. The initial alluring story lost its shine as the simple concrete actions it promoted failed to translate into real-world solutions.

Teachers, each day faced with the idea's inadequacy for resolving the fundamental problems of schooling, were among the first to speak out. Individuals, especially those active on social media, played a role in challenging data's dominance. They collectively gave voice to a frustration that many felt, but few were able to articulate. At first this voice fell on deaf ears as data was so embedded in formal systems of school improvement and accountability. It is hard to admit that we did something that did not work or was a waste of time. Not everyone felt these frustrations: for school improvement charities and companies that had bet their livelihoods on data, admitting the emperor has no clothes was not an option. But for school leaders trying to carry on regardless, momentum was increasingly hard to maintain in the face of growing dissatisfaction from teachers, research showing the invalidity of data processes and surveys reporting the enormous workload burden of data.[104]

And as levels of disquiet at the chalkface grew, the English education system was fortunate that its institutional structures were primed towards making a *volte-face*. For the most important coercive force in driving change within schools is Her Majesty's Chief Inspector, a political appointment that leads the schools' inspectorate. And with every newly appointed Chief Inspector comes the opportunity to mark a new chapter, which Amanda Spielman did with force in 2019 in a speech that gave a warning to schools:

> *If someone shows you a great big spreadsheet, you might want to ask who pulled it together and for what purpose. Who does the data help? Does it add value beyond what you'd get from talking to a teacher or head of department? Was it worth the time taken out of the teacher's day to enter all those numbers?*[105]

Shortly afterwards, Ofsted announced that they would not be asking about or examining 'in-year assessment data', the very thing that the Raising Standards Leader role was created to deliver in schools. Data as a school improvement tool was clearly in retreat and, while schools have been permanently changed by what happened to them, the fantastical attempts to measure learning have shifted once more – shifted, not declined, for the very nature of the fundamental problems in schooling is that we will find ourselves trying to fix them again and again. In the triumph of hope over experience, the system tends towards a serially monogamous relationship with ill-fated solutions and mandatory miracles. Each is eventually abandoned as it fails to live up to early promise, only to be immediately replaced by the next in a long line of potential suitors.

Searing memories and the Next Big Thing

We have previously noted the phenomena of the metamorphic problem. This is where an emerging problem (or, at least, the reconceptualisation of a persistent problem) bears the hallmarks of the previous solution. For example, attempts to solve educational problems via personalisation itself gave rise to problems that invited the next solution – data. Equally, as we will see in the next chapter, using data to solve educational problems eventually gives rise to the new solution. What is the mechanism by which this metamorphosis – from solution, to problem, to the next solution – occurs?

Perhaps the answer lies to some extent in 'the doctrine of the searing memory', proposed by Lord Burns, former chief economic adviser and permanent secretary to the UK Treasury. The idea is that there will be a painful, searing memory of the unintended consequences of an economic policy that will influence the consequent policies. For example, the mass unemployment of the 1930s spawned a commitment to avoid this at all costs in the future, which gave rise to Keynesian economic policies that were pursued in the following decades.[106]

What are the searing memories from the data wave? For teachers, it is perhaps the excessive workload and sense of disempowerment brought about by the outcomes of their efforts being codified and used to hold them accountable for things they only partly controlled. For school leaders, the searing memory may be of how their roles were steered towards data analysis and generating evidence of standards, a role quite removed from that which made them aspire to senior management. Perhaps even for Ofsted, the data wave created searing memories of the existential doubt caused when schools would show inspectors the carefully crafted, but unverifiable, internal data to prove pupil progress. For each party, the unintended consequences of the data solution created painful memories that would in turn invite remedy. As Michael Blastland puts it: 'Intensity often seems to invite clarity, which goes hand in hand with conviction, followed keenly by resolution: "Never again!"'[107]

The conviction that would arise from the searing memories of the data wave was that a return to the craft of teaching and a rejection of bureaucracy was required. Abstraction brought about by codification of learning, and the validity of capturing small progress steps, were to be rejected in favour of a solution that felt more authentic and concrete. The curriculum, and its pedagogical sister movements inspired by cognitive science, would be the solution to this latest conception of the fundamental problems of schooling. This solution offered an emphasis on teachers' professional judgement around curriculum construction, real-time feedback to assure pupils' understanding rather than delayed marking of work, a rejection of objective measures of school standards in favour of an aesthetic appreciation of beautiful curricula, a semi-scientific justification for classroom practice and a concrete conception of progress as being what pupils retained in long-term memory. It is no coincidence that the favoured solution happens to soothe most of the wounds left open by our previous attempts to resolve the fundamental problems of schooling. Of course, this latest solution will also leave its searing memories. In this way, our continuous attempts to find solutions to irresolvable problems will contribute to the re-imagining of the problem, from which the Next Big Thing will emerge.

Complex advice

Great big spreadsheets became the hallmark of an ill-fated data solution to the fundamental problems of schooling, the latest sticky idea. It is easy to be taken in by such appealingly simple solutions, then to switch our allegiance to the Next Big Thing.

To develop a healthy wariness of attractive educational solutions, we suggest:

1. Question who is advocating for this latest solution. What might their motivations be?
2. Remember that complex systems are not amenable to being solved. If something promises to do so, treat it with caution.
3. Be wary of attempts to codify and simplify processes. Explore the complexity of processes and mechanisms that could plausibly lead to successful outcomes.
4. Consider what 'searing memories' you have to which your response was 'never again'.

Reflective questions

- How attractive did you find the data solution? What was appealing or repulsive to you?
- Why is the narrative of 'closing gaps' so powerful in education? Why does it appeal to those working in schools?
- What spreadsheets and flight paths models have you used (or even developed)? What assumptions were these based on?
- Why do some schools appear reticent to scale back data collection?
- Who was empowered and who was disempowered by the proliferation of data in schools?

CHAPTER 6 – RIDING THE CURRICULUM WAVE

The waves fell; withdrew and fell again, like the thud
of a great beast stamping.

Virginia Woolf, *The Waves*[108]

Spending time in a teacher's lesson will always raise questions that, in turn, reflect the prevailing orthodoxy in education. Not so long ago, as a headteacher visiting lessons, Matthew would be interested to know which students were falling behind, what intervention had been employed to address this and how this had affected the progress of the class. By late 2019, he was armed with new questions, this time about the object of study, rather than the progress of individuals. At the forefront of his mind were curriculum questions, formulated through his reading of the likes of Christine Counsell, Mary Myatt and Michael F.D. Young, and given weight and urgency by Ofsted's renewed emphasis on the 'substance' of the curriculum. The questions: Why this? Why now? What purpose does this content serve in the curriculum? Where will it take the students?

A particular Year 8 geography lesson on waves is prominent in Matthew's memory. With the help of a diagram, the teacher explained the 'anatomy' of a wave to the class: crest, trough, wavelength and frequency. What purpose did this knowledge serve in helping to complete a geographical picture of the world? Links to science were immediately apparent and Matthew wondered whether students had already encountered wave concepts elsewhere in the curriculum. Was this an opportunity for his school to strengthen cross-disciplinary connections? His interest piqued, Matthew went away to learn more about waves and their place in the school curriculum. Perhaps surprisingly, he found that sea waves are not explicitly mentioned in the geography national curriculum at key stage 3 or before. Indeed, the three of us cannot remember being taught about waves at school: they were either absent from our own schools' curricula or our memories of the lessons have since been lost to time. What was behind the decision to teach the anatomy of a wave to these students?

If all you have is a hammer...

Curriculum questions fascinate educationalists because they tug at the big question: what are schools for? Are we teaching children about waves so that they develop a deeper understanding of the world in which they live? Will it inspire them to want to study and work in geographical fields? Will introducing waves at key stage 3 help children in future examinations? How will learning about a wave's form, characteristics and behaviour help students understand how they are used as a metaphorical language across other disciplines and literature?

Humans love to watch waves because they are soothingly regular, and yet unpredictably unique in the way they emerge, rise, peak, crash and shrink away to a mere memory. Education policy waves – of which personalisation and data were two – follow the same emergent pattern, with each policy wave being uniquely shaped by the strength, duration and journey of the collection of individual actors who choose to join it as it gathers strength.

Policy waves always start small, with a few suitors theorising about, debating and operationalising just one small area of education. There are teachers, academics and other educationalists who have devoted their careers to thinking about curriculum, even in the times when these ideas were not in vogue. And because, like each of us, they tend to construct self-narratives and solutions that are premised on the significance of their own area of expertise and imagined action, they believe curriculum change can be transformational. As the psychologist Abraham Maslow remarked, 'If the only tool you have is a hammer, it is tempting to treat everything as if it were a nail.'[109] For these curriculum suitors, they may feel like the last revolution has finally arrived.

The British sociologist Michael F.D. Young is certainly one of these curriculum suitors, having throughout his career argued for the centrality of curriculum in creating and perpetuating inequalities in education. At the start of Young's academic career in the 1970s, he edited what became a seminal sociological text, *Knowledge and Control*, that included chapters by academic giants such as Basil Bernstein and Pierre Bourdieu.[110] Together this 'new sociology of education' movement argued that the academic school curriculum, historically constructed to teach 'the knowledge of the powerful' and thus preserve the status quo of a class society, systematically ensured that most working-class pupils were failures. Their words were the inspiration for pedagogic strategies designed to suppress hierarchy, such as facilitation, group work and 'teaching as a conversation'.[111] The new sociology of education movement contributed to a knowledge revolution on both sides of the Atlantic, with widespread enthusiasm for integrated curricula courses such as environment or media studies that made schooling more relevant to the lives of children today. The ideas, as defined by Shoemaker, sound compelling:

> *[An integrated curriculum is] organised in such a way that it cuts across subject-matter lines, bringing together various aspects of the curriculum into meaningful association to focus upon broad areas of study. It views learning and teaching in a holistic way and reflects the real world, which is interactive.*[112]

Who could disagree that a curriculum should be connected rather than fragmented, immersive rather than detached, synergistic rather than discontinuous, shared rather than imposed? Proponents argued their curriculum reforms were consistent with the works of educational psychologists who theorise how children construct and come to learn new ideas. And by making education more relevant to students, engagement would rise, and dropout rates would fall. This, sadly, did not come to pass.

By 2007, Young was still arguing that construction of the school curriculum can perpetuate, or disrupt, social inequalities in attainment. However, his arguments had shifted largely as a result of watching his own children's education.[113] He published *Bringing Knowledge Back In*, a book extensively used by Conservative politicians to shape the curriculum reforms that restored the centrality of academic subjects in schools.[114] Along with the American E.D. Hirsch,[115] Young argued that educational inequalities among children are, fundamentally, inequalities in knowledge.[116] Rather than attend to children's existing interests, schools must teach things that children cannot learn elsewhere, so called 'powerful knowledge'.[117] Otherwise, there is no point in them. These types of broad-reaching arguments were like catnip to educationalists and policymakers who were looking for a new solution to close attainment gaps after the demise of personalisation, datafication and interventions. The curriculum wave began to swell.

Illusions of explanatory depth

It is hard to explain exactly how policy waves begin and grow because there is rarely systematic organisation of the actors involved. As we described in the last chapter, the policy wave is better thought of as *emergent* rather than imposed on the system by individuals. To thrive outside of their native habitat, ideas like Young's 'powerful knowledge' need to replicate quickly and offer something of value to many. Simplicity and ambitious aims are rewarded. Powerful knowledge offered both. No *one* person – not Michael Gove and certainly not Michael F.D. Young – was responsible for the late 2010s rise of the curriculum as a solution to under-achievement of children. Curriculum has been on a complex policy journey from Young's academic work, through early speeches by Nick Gibb, the 2014 national curriculum and new examination specifications, through to Amanda Spielman's 2019 inspection framework that places curriculum at its heart.

It feels like classroom teachers are more willing actors in the coalition of advocates for this curriculum wave, compared to other recent waves. While teachers often experience policy waves as something done to them, with their goal being to minimise the hassle of the latest fad, many teachers are attracted to the utility of reviewing and refining the content, sequence, resources and explanations that shape their day-to-day activities in the classroom. In contrast to the solutions endorsed during peak datafication, this emphasis upon powerful knowledge appeals to teachers' imagined realm of action – the classroom, and what they think proper teaching should be able to achieve. It allows teachers to focus on the things many say they love and find inherently rewarding, such as curriculum design, resource creation and lesson planning.

The curriculum offers everyone a simple, compelling explanation of the problem with schooling. Students deserve a high-quality curriculum, particularly those who are less likely to encounter powerful knowledge in other spheres of their lives. Envisaging a process that we are superficially familiar with is liable to induce a particular cognitive bias: the illusion of explanatory depth (IOED). This bias causes us to conflate familiarity with a process that we can easily visualise or mentally animate, with a detailed mechanistic understanding of how it actually works. It can be sparked by the flash of insight that an abstracted explanation provokes. The psychologist Frank Keil refers to this as the 'aha' moment. There is a rush of understanding when we first see how a particular explanation could fit together. However, this intuition is often misleading because, in reality, our understanding is less complete (or shallower) than we have come to believe.

> *People ... seem to use misleading heuristics to assess how well they understand a system. Most notably, if they can see or easily visualise several components of a system, they are more convinced they know how it works. Thus, the more easily visible are parts in a system, relative to hidden ones, the stronger the illusion of explanatory depth.*
>
> Frank Keil, writing in 2006 on
> explanation and understanding[118]

Aha! Of course, that makes sense. To ensure that students all make progress we need to design a curriculum that ensures they learn the (most) powerful knowledge available within each academic discipline. This requires both careful selection of content and sequencing to ensure that subsequent lessons build on and reinforce earlier learning. This classroom solution is easy to superficially imagine and so we overlook the lack of clearly set out mechanisms. Pre-existing beliefs may also lower the threshold of acceptance of these new explanations.[119] The curriculum wave aligns neatly with our imagined role of the teacher and their classroom, homogenising the students involved into a single entity 'the class', a limitation that we explored in chapter 3. The imagined, the intended, the enacted and the learned curriculum all merge into one as we persuade ourselves that transforming life chances is finally possible.

The popularity of curriculum reform as an instrument for school improvement today is clear. Books have been written, INSETs delivered, policy documents revised, inspection frameworks reformed. The wave has risen and is hurtling towards the shoreline. It is hard to find anyone who dares argue against its importance and transformative power, not politicians, regulators, trade unionists, headteachers or teachers. Just as data reform gained a faux solidarity through the language of flight paths and targets, so curriculum is developing its own catchphrases, such as 'The Curriculum is the Progression Model' to bat away the fundamental problems of schooling. Progress is simple: a student makes progress if they learn the curriculum. The phrase was first proposed in a blog in 2017 by Michael Fordham, a history teacher,[120] brought to prominence in 2018 by the influential policy expert Christine Counsell,[121] used in Ofsted policy documents by 2020[122] and is already on the website of dozens of schools to explain their approach to the fundamental problem of measuring learning and demonstrating impact.

This is not to say that everyone has jumped aboard the knowledge-led curriculum movement. As with the earlier data wave, quasi-mandatory coercion will pull many aboard, but others will quietly ignore the movement and continue as they have always done. In the main, until the wave peaks it is not expedient for many within the system to publicly question the outcomes that it promises.

The destructive force of genericism

Education policymakers' perennial search for generic solutions, and their validation by transient coalitions of advocates, generates successive failed policy waves. Promising ideas are distorted when granted a temporary monopoly for explaining and 'fixing' the entire system. Curriculum has been promoted to a lofty, but precarious and therefore inevitably transient position, as the latest 'answer' to the fundamental problems of schooling. We fear for the development of destructive tendencies for three reasons: genericism, collision with accountability and an under-appreciation of the status quo.

The policymakers' role includes a duty to close attainment gaps or raise school quality across the system. This leads them to seek transformative solutions, those that alluringly promise improvements by altering activities across every classroom, regardless of subject or phase expertise. Thus, policy waves are always propelled by powerful and persuasive language that appears to offer a generic solution: whole-school improvement. This requires the curriculum solution to be defined broadly enough that every teacher, regardless of what and who they teach, can join the reform movement.

Every movement develops a generic language to describe what must be done, and curriculum is no exception. The description of curriculum as 'the progression model' exemplifies this. This language quickly filters into language of Ofsted frameworks, DfE documents, school policies and generic training courses. However, any selected language is likely to resonate better in some subjects than others. Michael F.D. Young's phrase 'powerful knowledge' has become the rallying cry around which curriculum reformers gather. The curriculum, he argues, should teach this powerful knowledge:

> We want schools to give children access to knowledge that takes them beyond their experience in a way that their parents can trust and value, that they will find challenging, and which prepares them for the next step in their education.
>
> Michael F.D. Young, writing in the 2014
> *Knowledge and the Future School*[123]

In some subjects the phrase 'powerful knowledge' is meaningful to teachers and can provide them with a clear guide for what should be taught. For example, teaching children the science behind waves and the technical language to describe them is powerful knowledge; experiencing waves in person on the coastline might *feel* powerful, but it is not powerful knowledge. Equally, understanding the inter-relationship of the split of the Church of England with Rome and the lives of the Tudor kings and queens is powerful knowledge; learning what sorts of clothes Henry VIII wore is likely not. However, even here it is plausible that different history departments could identify entirely different packets of powerful knowledge to convey to their students.

In other contexts, powerful knowledge fails to signal what teachers instinctively feel is valuable and important and does not convey useful ideas about what should be taught. What is the powerful knowledge in the primary maths curriculum? Proponents of powerful knowledge say it is distinct from 'common sense' knowledge acquired through everyday experience, so is the powerful knowledge learning about vectors and algebra, rather than arithmetic that can be picked up in everyday working life as well as in the education system? Perhaps it is, but secondary maths teachers would argue that this conflicts with the most important tools that 11-year-olds (often fail to) master.

There are many other phrases that resonate in some subjects – usually the ones with cumulative and therefore more contentious knowledge domains – but not in others. In the hierarchical subjects, such as maths and foreign-language learning, where mastery is critical to progress, it can be quite damaging to develop curricula that are 'ambitious', 'an inch deep and mile wide' with 'teaching to the top' and using the 'curriculum as the progression model'. Indeed, even words such as 'knowing', 'experiencing', 'learning', 'understanding' and 'doing' hold different meanings across different subjects due to variation in intrinsic knowledge structures and the cultural regularities of the subject community.

Similarly, the generic implementation of curriculum reform has led to tools such as knowledge organisers that can be very helpful in many subjects where they explicitly set out knowledge to be learned, but not in others such as maths because they lend themselves poorly to procedural knowledge.[124] And if schools develop policies where knowledge organisers should be used as the core of the homework strategy across departments, as some have, it will be suboptimal for many disciplines. The same is true for curriculum maps, retrieval practice quizzes and other strategies that have been imposed on teachers.

The generic enactment of the curriculum reform movement is quite ironic, given that its suitors are, by definition, committed to complex and nuanced debates about the nature of knowledge across different subjects. But the policy wave no longer belongs to them. It has long since been taken up by the coalition of advocates who have much greater ambitions for what it might achieve. But in promoting these ambitions they inevitably, alas, diminish the possibility of the movement achieving valuable change.

Collision with accountability

Internal systems of monitoring are inevitably mirrored by external systems of accountability. Attending to the curriculum is no different. Curriculum quality has been placed at the heart of evaluation in the new Ofsted framework and so school internal processes must be reviewed with this external evaluation in mind. When school departments complete an evaluation of their curricula at the end of the year, will this be an evaluation to support improvement or an evaluation to rationalise and evidence that it is already 'good' or 'outstanding'? Surely it cannot be both at once? Activities to 'prove' that curriculum reform has worked have already begun in schools. Regardless of the domain, accountability always discourages nuanced self-evaluation and improvement in favour of evidencing success.

The nature of the damage that accountability imposes on school practice somewhat depends on whether the policy wave becomes a *mandatory miracle* or an *ill-fated solution*. We described personalisation as a mandatory miracle because the call to action contained no specific instructions as to what should be done. We described datafication as an ill-fated solution because the call to action contained very specific instructions, albeit ones with no mechanism by which attainment would improve. The three of us are still unsure whether curriculum will turn out to be a mandatory miracle or an ill-fated solution. It will largely depend on how Ofsted develops further guidance about exactly what is expected of schools. While we see some glimmers of ill-fated solutions, in the form of compulsory curriculum maps and knowledge organisers, for the most part this policy wave currently seems to have miraculous qualities, with teachers enacting all sorts of curious changes in the name of curriculum reform. Many of these could be classified as what Dylan Wiliam called 'lethal mutations'; good ideas that are implemented in ways that render them ineffective or even counter-productive.[125]

For example, one head of RE was recently asked to restructure her curriculum to focus on careers, as that was 'what Ofsted wanted'. This entailed the creation of a scheme of work arranged thematically by different areas of employment rather than by categories or topics native to the domain of religious studies. The 'Wedding at Cana' miracle, where Jesus turns water into wine and that Christians read as an indication of both his divinity and messianic status, was moved out of 'Christian Beliefs and Teachings' and into an 'Events Management' themed unit! It would be funny were it not true.

In the above example, the curriculum wave has reached the level of a cargo cult. Cargo cult refers to the belief that developed in a Melanesian tribe that building runways would bring about the arrival of a miraculous 'cargo' of goods from supernatural sources, based on the observation of supplies being delivered by aircraft to colonial officials.[126] Such activity is at the expense of traditional uses of materials and the observance of local customs and social and economic activity. In a similar way, the beliefs concerning 'what Ofsted want' and the impression that a policy or practice is widespread can give it a momentum of its own, in the belief that precious rewards will follow. No one, especially not Ofsted's chief inspector, was hoping for a surge in career-themed theological curricular content. But such outcomes can and will continue to emerge.

Under-appreciation of the status quo

More than 40 years ago, curriculum expert Lawrence Stenhouse wrote sagely: 'The central problem of curriculum study is the gap between our ideas and aspirations and our attempt to operationalise them.'[127] Our curriculum wave is still quite young and so enormous energy is being put into constructing an ideal or intended curriculum for schools. These can be beautiful documents, setting out our ideals of what children should learn and how knowledge structures should fit together. They describe our aspirations for what students might learn tomorrow in relation to what they should have learned in the past. They fixate on the belief that there is a perfect sequence of knowledge acquisition.[128] However, the simplicity of these documents quickly crumbles as it gets enacted in the complexity of the classroom, where the teacher's vision of a lesson rarely matches the students' recollection of it and where more knowledge is forgotten than remembered. It is in the messiness of the classroom that we will be rudely awakened by the complexity of the compromised curriculum where perfect knowledge mapping is displaced by 30 brains with utterly different prior knowledge, or at least recollection of prior knowledge. So much so that the intended curriculum and the enacted curriculum may end up so far apart that we cannot use our hoped for ends of the former to justify disruption to the latter.

Disrupting a complex system means disrupting a set of habits, beliefs, resources and practices. If these are not fully understood you will inevitably underestimate the scale of the challenge and so curriculum reform will fail because it does not change much. Or worse, it will fail and in doing so will make a stable, though very imperfect, curriculum into a highly unstable and chaotic one. One example is the curious nature of 'the afternoon' in primary schools, a phrase often used as a euphemism for the part of the day when pupils do something other than the 3Rs. To the untrained eye of an outsider such as a secondary teacher, the activities in the afternoon can seem quite strange. Even primary teachers can find it quite hard to articulate why afternoons are organised the way they are. However, long-standing practices persist for a reason, even if that reason is rather oblique. It is critical that we are not dismissive of the status quo before we try to disrupt it.

Implementing complex reforms at speed, and alone, is often likely to deliver a solution worse than its less-than-perfect predecessor. We saw the results of this in the byzantine systems that schools implemented to replace national curriculum levels. This happened when headteachers needed to implement an assessment and data monitoring system within weeks rather than years. Now these failed systems are being replaced by the mantra that the curriculum can be the progression model, implying we can simply tick off the knowledge as it is delivered. But the simplicity of our latest solution will be disrupted by students who inevitably 'progress' at different speeds and make sense of identical lessons in a multiplicity of ways.

The end is the beginning

We are surfers reaching the crest of a wave and momentarily feeling that we can ride it forever. Alas, one day *all* waves must crash. Policy waves lose energy through their frictional encounter with the shoreline of schools going about their daily lives. How they hit the shoreline depends on whether they are small constructive waves, gently bringing new ideas to schools, or large destructive waves that damage shorelines through the energy of their arrival. The curriculum wave could have remained 'low energy' if it had remained the activities of subject specialists working on incremental improvements within their discipline. However, once taken up by politicians and Ofsted and spun into a perfect solution capable of fixing the curriculum across all subjects and phases with the goal of closing the attainment gap, destruction becomes inevitable.

That said, the curriculum wave is still gaining energy and we have no crystal ball into which we can see how it ultimately lands on our shoreline as it gets enacted in the classroom. Should we be fearful of what lies ahead?

We think there are already enough early warning signs to show us how and why the curriculum policy wave will crash. For while its surface narrative is alluring, in practice it is ill-defined without consensus on how its aims can be realised. This poor specification is caused by a weak evidence base from which the movement was launched *and*, ultimately, the reason why systematic policy evaluation of the movement is never possible.[129] We will never clearly determine the benefits the curriculum wave brought with it, the sediment it left behind or the quality of the material it washed away. The curriculum wave cannot solve the fundamental problems of schooling, and even if it could make a difference, we would struggle to determine if it had.

Is it within our gift to collectively work to stop the crash happening? We don't think we can. We could promote an objective critique of the curriculum wave and seek to scale it back to make it once again a localised, constructive solution to specific problems, but virtue signalling means it takes a brave soul to criticise any proposed 'universal' solution to the attainment gap, even an unevidenced and implausible one. Those who propose solutions are always virtuous because they clearly care about a problem we must solve. Those who suggest the solution will not work, and who have no better solution, are denying the problem the opportunity of the resolution it so desperately needs.

However, we believe that the curriculum wave, like most waves to varying degrees, has served a purpose, and is moving the system forward in some beneficial ways. It has proven an antidote to the data that flooded schools for a period, which we see as a far more destructive wave than the current curriculum one. A powerful wash *was* needed to sweep away a considerable amount of harmful practice and the cleansing effect of focusing on what should be taught, rather than the abstract attempt to crudely codify what has been learned, has been far more empowering for teachers.

It is also good, in our view, that we have been reminded of the importance of subjects and disciplinary traditions. These structures provide stability, helping form a clear identity for secondary teachers at least, locating them within a community of practice. This, in turn, reinforces traditions that mitigate against whimsical reform. A focus on the curriculum has also brought to the fore some fundamental concepts in curriculum design, such as knowledge structures, and some empirically important pedagogical ideas, such as the importance of retrieval practice in securing knowledge in long-term memory. Teachers' understanding of such concepts by no means guarantees more effective classroom practice, but they are an important part of a teacher's professional knowledge.

Given where we are now, how might we ensure that the curriculum wave is as constructive as possible – that the sediment left behind is beneficial? Ironically, we should take the strength out of this wave by reducing its energy and momentum. But how? First, we must not seize upon curriculum reform as the solution to everything. Second, we should be specific about exactly what problems we are trying to solve in our schools that may benefit from curriculum innovation. Third, we should slow down. Reform will be most constructive if it avoids sweeping away everything in its path – if it enhances rather than replaces the well-established procedural regularities that enable the school to function. Neither policymakers nor school leaders, as we shall see in the chapters to come, truly comprehend the delicacy, nuance or diversity of the school, therefore genuine and sustainable school improvement requires collective sense making by engaging those on whose behavioural changes it relies.

There will be sediment from the data wave that should remain – lessons learned about how we assess and record learning gains (and how not to do it). There are areas where data is helpful, such as the online maths platforms that promote deliberate practice and direct pupils towards addressing error and misunderstanding. It is not that we should seek to remove data from schools, but rather we find specific and constructive uses for it. Similarly, we might wish to retain some habitual practices, such as the intermittent moments where teachers pause and reflect on which children are on track and which are falling behind, which the data-drop cycles did so simplistically and rigidly, but that may be adapted to become more professionally useful. We are learning that datafication is not everything, but it can serve some purpose. So too may we learn that curriculum thinking is not a silver bullet, but it is a weapon in our armoury.

Policy waves are inevitable, and we cannot prevent their emergence nor their crash. While it is not possible to conceive of what form the next wave after curriculum will take, we can predict that it will gain momentum as it promises to address the flaws in the current orthodoxy and be sufficiently appealing to a coalition of advocates. Ill-fated solutions and mandatory miracles are compelling because they create a narrative using persuasive language, but they are naïvely simplistic and extend a solution further than it is ever possible to take it. We can learn to be watchful for waves and to be wary of their appeal and undeliverable promises. Perhaps we can learn to harness waves in more constructive ways by not fooling ourselves that we will ride any particular wave forever.

Once we understand the anatomy of waves and their origins, we may be dispirited by our apparent impotence in relation to such powerful, systemic forces. We seem so easily taken in by the promise and appeal of ultimately ill-fated solutions. It is perhaps easier to remain in a state of denial, riding each wave that comes along, believing it will last forever. Like the surfer, it is tiring to repeatedly topple into the sea, then climb aboard once more in anticipation of the next wave. However, we contend that confronting the true complexity of our education system will make us wiser and our actions more realistic and informed. With this in mind, we will venture further into understanding the diversity and unpredictability of schools in a belief that with clearer insight comes more effective action.

Complex advice

The current preoccupation with curriculum, like all policy waves, will pass. In the meantime, we should make this wave as constructive as possible, ensuring it leaves behind it some beneficial sediment.

To take the best from the curriculum wave we suggest the following:

1. Think carefully about what you place in the curriculum but avoid over-reliance on a single frame of reference for this choice, such as selecting only the powerful knowledge, teaching only what is likely to be in the exam or making every topic relevant to the child's future life.
2. Avoid fixating on the curriculum as the solution to almost every problem. Without good behaviour and pedagogy, a perfect curriculum roadmap will remain a curriculum roadmap and little more.
3. If you are in a position to tell teachers what to do, know that there is no bolt-on technique or method, be it knowledge organisers or retrieval practice, which should be applied across the curriculum.
4. Do not be tempted to take the logic of one discipline and apply it across the whole system.
5. Put your proposals for curriculum reform under scrutiny by a range of people with different expertise and perspectives.

Reflective questions

- Can the inclusion of any one topic or concept in the curriculum be attributed to serving a singular purpose? How do those who choose curriculum content justify its inclusion?
- What language is used in your school to talk about the curriculum? To what extent is there a shared understanding of this language? What does its use reveal about the beliefs and assumptions of those who use it?
- What distortions of practice have you observed that are justified as 'what Ofsted want', or by a claim that this is what other schools are doing?
- Is the curriculum wave a mandated miracle, an ill-fated solution, or neither?
- What beneficial sediment has been left behind by the data wave in your context?

CHAPTER 7 – THE HIDDEN LIVES OF TEACHERS

The Secret Garden was what Mary called it when she was thinking of it. She liked the name, and she liked still more the feeling that when its beautiful old walls shut her in no one knew where she was.

Frances Hodgson Burnett, *The Secret Garden*[130]

It is quarter past four on a Monday afternoon in 2014 and the teaching staff of one secondary school are in a training session. The speaker is explaining that it is essential that every child makes progress within a lesson and that this entails producing class information sheets to ensure that sub-groups of students are effectively targeted. The teachers present are each hearing (and learning) something different.

Jane, a newly qualified maths teacher, is busily taking notes. She is also worrying about Class 10C who she teaches for a double lesson tomorrow. Particularly those three students who are almost out of control. Why did her mentor have to pick this class for her fortnightly observation, she wonders? Her lesson plan is not yet written, and after tonight's session she fears she will now be asked to show that every child is making progress – even the three troublemakers. It will be another late night.

Lucas is not taking notes. It might look like he is as he types away on his laptop, but he is marking ICT coursework ahead of the looming submission deadline.

Morgan, a senior leader in charge of teaching and learning, is sat in the sparsely populated front row hoping that the session helps improve the limited embedding of formative assessment that Ofsted highlighted in their last visit. The inspectorate's return is overdue.

Paula, who teaches psychology, is listening attentively but is far from convinced. She is troubled by the latest trend for glitzy activities and a palpable buzz in lessons as it is entirely at odds with the way she has been teaching for the past two decades. Maybe she does need to jazz things up a bit. Maybe she is not cut out for the job anymore. If she does stay, she will need to learn about these new hoops and how to jump through them – at least while the observer is in the room.

Professional looseness

In chapter 3, we discussed Graham Nuthall's seminal work in which he revealed the hidden lives of learners: the diverse and individual journeys children go on as they experience school lessons, and the unexpected ways this impacts upon them.[131] Teachers live hidden lives too, tucked inside classrooms, navigating their own diverse and unique journeys through the education system. The isolation of teachers means that their diversity is rarely diminished, despite the desires of school leaders and policymakers, contributing to complexity within the school system.

At first glance, classrooms have a surface level simplicity that is well understood by everyone in society who has been in one. Classrooms are rooms where bundles of children are placed with a knowledgeable adult for about five hours of instructional time each day. However, this surface level simplicity belies considerable diversity of classroom practice. Peering into classrooms across England, we will observe hundreds of different questioning strategies, thousands of different techniques for motivating children, numerous ways of encouraging student collaboration and dozens of approaches to using the same resources. Moreover, schools themselves are diverse in the policies and procedures they adopt. We are a country of approximately 18,000 different behaviour policies, marking and feedback protocols, reporting procedures and so on. And though we have a national curriculum, it still yields about 10,000 different versions of Year 4 history. Even where teachers are preparing students for a particular qualification, say AQA English Literature, there are still hundreds of different instructional responses to the one specification.

Some of this diversity is deliberate, the result of teachers considering the task ahead of them and consciously selecting the approach or tool they deem most appropriate. They make different decisions to one another, in part, due to the diversity of beliefs they hold about every facet of teaching. From beliefs about the purpose of education, through to optimal pedagogy and behavioural management approaches, there really is no such thing as a typical teacher. For example, 48% of teachers are authoritarian in their stance towards pupil behaviour, saying that they believe in zero tolerance, yet 10% say we should never exclude a student from school.[132] A total of 61% of teachers think students learn best when they discover things for themselves; 27% disagree.[133] A figure of 40% of teachers do not believe their own opinion is any more valid than that of their students; 48% disagree.[134] A total of 71% feel that the purpose of education is to prepare children for the world of work; 22% disagree.[135]

There is significant variety in what teachers do each day, in what they believe society requires them to do, in what drives their actions and in what is stopping them from doing things differently. This diversity makes teaching a peculiarly nebulous profession. Teachers are professionals in that they engage in structured training and achieve formal qualifications. Teachers are professionals in that they seek to apply their knowledge and skills in the interest of others in society. Yet there is not a defined body of knowledge, agreed procedural regularity or code of practice and ethics to which all teachers subscribe. Contrast teaching with architecture, accountancy, even acting and we reveal the comparative looseness within the practice of teaching, and the contested nature of how teaching professionals are expected to perform their role.

Whenever you hear someone say, 'But no teacher believes that…', they inevitably do. Very little is known about *why* teachers develop such a range of views on the essence, purpose and impact of teaching. For while it is obvious that differences in subject matter between drama and maths might lead to different teacher beliefs about their work, this does not explain why drama teachers are so different from one another in their beliefs and actions. We all develop our notions of what teaching should be at a very young age, while watching our own teachers. And we supplement these nascent ideas about teaching with new arguments about how the job should be done, each time choosing to assimilate the new ideas that fit most comfortably with how we already do the job we do. These disparate beliefs constitute a filter through which new information and directives are interpreted, explaining why new policy initiatives resonate differently across the profession.

Beliefs shape the *deliberate* choices that teachers make as they go about their daily lives, but habits are more important in shaping much of what is done in the classroom. Diversity in these habitual behaviours is equally important in explaining why teachers are so different to one another.

As anyone involved in attempts to change teacher behaviours at school at the local or national level will have learned, teacher habits are diverse, strong and resistant to change. All effective teachers are creatures of habit. These habits are the repertoire of teaching techniques that have been repeated so many times that they have been consolidated in their long-term memory, thus becoming automated and therefore insensitive to feedback. Habituated behaviours require little or no conscious thought.

The habits of the classroom are needed to make teaching fluent, but they also actively stop teachers from adapting their practice to improve.[136] Deliberately changing behaviours is a costly act. Teachers' habituated behaviours are particularly resistant to change because they rely on little or no conscious thought. The cacophony of cognitive demands in the foreground of a classroom lesson leaves little capacity for modifying or changing a long-since entrenched and automated behavioural sequence.

These habits of the classroom are the reason why the educator Professor Dylan Wiliam says:

> *One of the most important things I have learned in thirty years as a teacher educator is that it is much easier to change what teachers do when students are not present than it is to change what they do when students are present.*[137]

Adaptive agents

When thinking about the teaching staff in a school, it is tempting for school leaders to conceive of teachers as the passive target of the latest new policy or professional development initiative. It is easy to imagine the school is one in which teachers teach in a largely similar manner, and downplay the distinctiveness of individuals' motivations, beliefs and habits. This is perhaps inevitable when one's role entails improving teaching and learning at scale. From this perspective, introducing and embedding a new approach is a matter of sharing the correct instructions and ensuring that staff are clear on the need to modify their practice in the light of it. Successful implementation is a volitional matter. Leaders need to sell the new initiative successfully. In some cases, they may need to coerce adoption by more overt and direct means.

The reality is far more complex. Teachers are adaptive agents, each responding independently and unpredictably to the changing dynamics of the school environment. Their responses and behaviours are constantly evolving as they receive information about the success or failure of their adaptations. Complexity scientist John Holland suggests that adaptive agents tend to act rationally, but that that this rationality is bounded.[138] Teachers will act in the way that is most efficient given the bounds of their knowledge, capacity, role and circumstance. Often this will involve not changing their behaviour or changing it in ways we do not expect.

By framing the school as a complex adaptive system with independently acting agents receiving new information that may or may not be useful to them, we can start to see why professional development sessions are invariably unsuccessful. Teachers are anything but passive recipients of a professional development session, initiative or policy. New demands, such as those expressed in the training session described above, are experienced not in isolation but amidst the noise of information that permeates their environment. Each teacher's interpretation and the behaviours that it may trigger will be shaped by both prior experiences and beliefs, the range of behaviours that they are capable of enacting and their capacity to innovate. While the teacher *may* attempt to alter their classroom practice initially to reflect what they are told they should do, over time they will experience whether this practice genuinely has efficacy for them in the classroom, and so weigh up the costs involved in replacing or disrupting their regular practices. If the net effect is disruptive, ineffective or the impact is simply ambiguous, they will be unlikely to continue with this adaptation. To survive or even thrive in this context, teachers need to develop a tacit understanding of the impossibility of meeting all the demands made of them. Adaptive compromises and fixes – both practical and psychological – allow them to maintain their own motivations, to keep calm and carry on.

The adaptations of agents within the system in turn drives the system itself to evolve, leading to new emergent regularities. For example, we may find the initial impact of widespread leadership observations of teaching fades over time as those subject to these observations develop adaptive strategies to satisfy those observing, while also being able to meet the complex demands of classroom teaching. The cultural norm therefore becomes to play the observation game, rather than to engage in developing one's practice meaningfully. And so, in addition to teaching expertise, teachers develop a compliancy expertise in signalling to management that they are 'on board' and a 'good teacher'. Compliancy expertise allows teachers to continue living their hidden lives.

Professional isolation

One of the things that forces workers to adopt similar practices, including those set out in professional development sessions, is the act of working alongside one another in a team. This happens in many professional lines of work, leading to firms or even whole professions adopting professional standards and practices that everyone must adhere to. Teaching does not need the prescriptive professional rulebook of other industries because teachers rarely work directly alongside one another in the classroom. And so, one reason why teacher practice is diverse is simply because it can be. Teachers' isolation is physical and practical, a product of busy timetables and four walls of their professional domain that are rarely breached by other professionals.

One paradox of teaching is that, while teachers spend their days in the crowded classroom, it can often be a rather lonely job. Teachers spend relatively little time with their teaching colleagues and many interactions they do have are rather superficial – the five second 'hello' in the corridor or the three minute chat by the photocopier. On any given day, 26% of teachers choose to eat lunch on their own and a further 8% skip lunch altogether (perhaps a function of the reduction in the length of lunch hours in many schools over the years and the work pressure that means teachers eat while they work).[139] Just 5% of teachers say they go to the pub with their colleagues most weeks; 12% say they have never gone.[140]

In describing the architecture and behaviour of complex systems, Herbert A. Simon observes that the extent of interaction between agents and sub-systems in an organisational hierarchy determines the 'decomposability' of the system.[141] His ideas show that where there are few interactions between parts of a system, the behaviours of these parts can be quite different from one another. He gives the example of a building with reasonably effective external and internal insulating walls. A thermometer hangs in each room and these show a wide variation in temperature from room to room – a state of thermal disequilibrium. How long will it take to achieve thermal equilibrium? This will depend on the effectiveness of the insulating walls (all else being equal). In other words, the stronger the barriers to interaction, the more resistant the system to equalisation. Equally, the greater the isolation of teachers, the greater the emergence of diverse classroom practice. So, while senior leaders with small teaching loads can easily achieve synergy of thought and practice by talking to their colleagues, classroom teachers cannot.

Often this isolation is actively sought by teachers; the US sociologist David Flinders describes teacher isolation itself as an adaptive strategy because it protects the time and energy required to meet instructional demands, allowing teachers an opportunity to recharge.[142] In addition to being practically adaptive, such isolation may have an existential benefit, allowing teachers to tell themselves contrasting but personally essential stories about their professional roles. It helps both teachers and leaders to avoid countenancing the complexity – impossibility even – of their roles and the disparate ways in which they muddle through with them.

Pressing change

It is now 4:55pm in the after-school meeting. The deputy head presents the new system for assessment and parental reporting that will replace the old one. They talk it through for 20 minutes, hand out the paperwork and then ask the magic question: 'Does anyone have any questions?' And inside the heads of almost every member of staff there is a little voice squeaking, 'Please don't ask any questions…Please don't ask any questions.' For, by now, these teachers have been working for well over eight hours in demanding conditions with little break. They are exhausted and their minds have turned to getting home, looking after their own family, catching up with their marking and planning the lessons they must teach the next day.

The US sociologist Seymour B. Sarason says that 'existing vehicles for discussion and planning [such as after-school teacher meetings] are based on the principle of the avoidance of controversy'.[143] Teachers fail to articulate that the new data policy created by the assistant heads makes no sense because the school day has no room for meetings that facilitate respectful and collaborative dialogue and planning. In England, one in 10 teachers say they are *never* able to participate in decisions that affect the nature of their job and one in five say that teachers are not able to raise problems and tough issues with management at their school.[144]

Not raising awkward questions sounds unhealthy but can be practically expedient, allowing a convenient fiction to be maintained. Teachers benefit from collectively deploying their compliance expertise. As a result, leaders *feel* that they are leading and implementing successful change (an illusion that we will return to in chapter 9). Teachers allow leaders to feel this and then go home to get on with their 'real' work.

The complexity and diversity of what teaching is in schools frustrates attempts to comprehend, let alone alter, the core processes of teaching and learning. Professional development sessions are rarely capable of sparking consistent and improved changes to teachers' practice, not because the sessions are of poor quality, but because they are based on an inadequate model of who teachers are and what they do. Where change *is* produced, the nature and net effect of this change is rarely clear or predictable. Even in retrospect, working out what happened and why is a tall order.

Never good enough

The teachers attending the after-school session on assessment and parental reporting may be keeping their heads down, not asking questions, but each of them feels, to some degree, that they are failing. The latest 'group information sheet' they are staring at, which requires progress reporting by prior attainment and specific needs – is intimidating and hard to countenance given how full a teaching day is. But it is troubling for a more existential reason: it presents teaching as a complicated, rather than a complex endeavour. It promises a solution, rather than acknowledging that the problem will persist beyond attempts to solve it. At this meeting, teachers are once again being told that the fundamental problems of schooling can be overcome, if only they do a better job in differentiating their instruction to match the needs of the individual students.

If only teachers were less isolated, with more room for professional dialogue with colleagues, they might better laugh off these initiatives. They may even recognise them for the ill-fated solutions or mandatory miracles that they often are. But it is all too easy for 'pluralistic ignorance' to take hold, with individual teachers erroneously inferring that they are the only one who has reservations about management's latest proposal.[145]

Here we see the issue created by bounded knowledge of each of our adaptive agents. Each likely understands *they* do not get teaching right, but they may be unaware that most other teachers experience the same problem. Most teachers feel the pressure of the infinite demands of the job that is placed on them. This is the case in specific teaching moments where the academic or behavioural demands made, simultaneously, by multiple children present an impossible challenge – one that necessitates compromise rather than affording neat resolution. It also applies to the longer term aims towards which teachers are working. Teachers must manage considerable job ambiguity. Should they be a curriculum designer? What about an instructor or a marker? Are they a resource creator? Must they also be a social worker or a counsellor?

A professional tension between expectation and reality is not unique to teaching, but it does seem to be particularly prominent in public services. In *Street-Level Bureaucracy*, Michael Lipsky explores the difficulties faced by social workers who must manage the dissonance between what is expected of them in their role (and indeed the ideals that attracted them to it) and the reality of limited resources, challenges inherent to changing behaviours and competing demands upon their time.[146] Similarly, if teachers are told that 'teaching changes lives',[147] should they feel they are a failure when they know a child they teach has not been transformed?

Teachers respond to this tension in a range of ways. But in the main this is a challenge that they navigate alone. In conducting workload interviews in secondary schools, Ben came across disparate distinct responses. One teacher, a recently promoted senior leader in a secondary school, took personal responsibility for failing to achieve what was expected of her:

> *I think most teachers feel guilt and responsibility. ...*
> *You're never finished, you can never be finished. It's*
> *never as good as you want it to be. There's always*
> *someone out there who seems to be doing it better*
> *than you. ...that idea of guilt...that sense that there's*
> *always something else that you can do to be better.*[148]

A second teacher described years of largely ignoring what he saw as unrealistic demands and unhelpful pedagogical directives, continuing to teach as he believed was best. He chose not to seek promotion, instead working as a classroom teacher for 15 years within the same school. His adaptation also seemed to come at an emotional cost:

> *I'm always waiting to be caught in the headlight. As I*
> *grow older it sort of...it's completely emotionally...it's*
> *not real because every day I have a positive emotional*
> *experience in school, but underneath it I have...a*
> *concern that one day I'm going to be found out for*
> *doing things the way that I do them.*[149]

Both these teachers found working in a school to be an emotionally challenging experience. However, they also talked enthusiastically about their jobs and the enjoyment they found in them. They were each able to construct a self-narrative in which their role was a meaningful one – despite the contradictions, challenges and management interventions that they experienced. So far, they had adapted to survive – even thrive – in their chosen profession.

Living with the fundamental problems of schooling

In her article, 'Parsing the practice of teaching', Mary Kennedy proposes that we focus our attention on the persistent problems experienced by teachers, those that cannot be fully resolved and that require compromises in relation to each demand and each individual student.[150] Her 'persistent problems' are manifestations of the fundamental problems of schooling and serve to create a job in which one can improve, but never fully master. Kennedy's final persistent problem in teaching is carefully balancing impossible (and persistent) demands in a sustainable way. As she says:

> *If a teacher cannot find a way to create an atmosphere that he or she is comfortable living in, he or she is not likely to remain teaching for very long.*[151]

Established habits help teachers considerably in this regard. These routinised set-pieces bring fluency to teaching and allow teachers to navigate each lesson on a more even keel than would otherwise be possible. But, beyond this, teachers must find a way to rationalise their lived experience against their beliefs about education's purpose while protecting their own sense of self-efficacy. Teachers also need to navigate their way through whole-staff training sessions!

At our school, it is past 5pm. Lucas wraps up marking his ICT coursework and scrawls in a group information sheet for his next lesson observation. As the meeting closes, he lets out a satisfied sigh, pleased to have cleared time to see his four-year-old daughter when he gets home.

Paula looks across at Lucas and wonders how he manages to let these constant missives wash over him without succumbing to worry. She makes a mental note to check in with him tomorrow morning. Maybe he will offer some wisdom.

Jane spends much of the evening carefully completing the information sheets requested and planning for her lesson observation. Perhaps Jane does fall out, again, with those troublesome Year 10s. But this time she notices something. There is a begrudging respect there from two of them. Despite their bravado, they apologise and try hard on their next tasks. Maybe the class is beginning to turn a corner. Maybe she can do the job after all.

Morgan smiles as Paula, Jane, Lucas and other staff thank him for arranging the training session. Morgan's needs have certainly been met by the session as he imagines the school can now transform teaching using the new approach.

A few weeks later, Asmitha asks Morgan if she can focus her whole-school National Professional Qualification for Senior Leadership (NPQSL) project on embedding formative assessment across the school. She would like to modify these group information sheets, as they do not currently flag up the full range of 'groups' that should be monitored.

As we leave the training session, we may reflect that each of these teachers is finding their own way in the job, eking out job satisfaction, reconciling the competing demands on their time and attention and perhaps finding pockets of joy in their hectic days.

A monitorial system for teacher learning?

Ill-fated solutions, as we explored in chapters 4 to 6, rest on naïve simplifications. Many of the initiatives 'delivered' via whole-staff training sessions probably fit this category. In a period marked by successive waves of generic policy solutions, responsibility for teaching and learning has migrated from teachers in their departments to school leaders, often given titles such as 'assistant head for teaching and learning'. From a senior leader's perspective, the observation that professional development sessions like this have negligible (at best) influence upon teaching behaviour in the long run indicates a failure. The inadequacy of such events for changing behaviour has been subject to considerable attention in recent years.

However, it is possible to view the after-school meetings that introduce the Next Big Thing as a useful, adaptive response to the external demand to align. It satisfies accountability partners and senior leaders with responsibility for the area while having only a moderate impact upon the daily teaching experience of most staff. This serves to protect teachers' hidden diversity and shelters them, to some degree, from the need to significantly alter their daily practice. However, this adaptation comes at a cost. Teacher isolation is compounded, and improvements to practice happen despite, not because of, professional development sessions.

The lock-step problem that is baked into our dominant model of schooling is as much a problem for our teachers who are trying to learn how to do their jobs as it is for the students they teach. Just as a lesson cannot be perfectly aligned with the needs of every individual in the class, producing those 'You Should Know This' moments, it is unlikely that en masse professional development for teachers can be well-aligned to their stage of development and capacities to improve. Alternatives to lock-step professional development in the form of instructional coaching mirror the advantages of the monitorial system we described in chapter 4, where the most experienced and advanced students assist the less advanced:

> *Instructional coaching involves an expert teacher working with a novice in an individualised, classroom-based, observation–feedback–practice cycle. Crucially, instructional coaching involves revisiting the same specific skills several times, with focused, bite-sized bits of feedback specifying not just what but* how *the novice needs to improve during each cycle.*
>
> Dr Sam Sims, writing in 2019[152]

This approach recognises teacher diversity and the challenges of producing sustained behavioural change to overcome habits of the classroom. As such, it seems better placed than a one-off genericised meeting to support individual teachers in finding, as Kennedy puts it, 'a way [of working] that is consistent with their own personalities and personal needs'.[153] Moreover, research suggests that instructional coaching can lead teachers to achieve small improvements in their efficiency within the complex classroom environment.[154]

However, the individualised approach to teacher learning is as expensive as the tutorial approach to student learning. The individual support required places far greater demands upon coaches' time than whole-staff meetings. And it cannot negate complexity and opaqueness of school purpose, particularly in the writing of the rubrics used for classroom observation that determine how teacher practice is judged. For we cannot write these rubrics without deciding exactly which areas require greater alignment of practice across classrooms, and in which we will allow teacher diversity to flourish. Good candidates for alignment are any areas where students need consistency in experience: safeguarding, behaviour management and lesson transitions in secondary schools being obvious candidates. Ironically, primary schools, where teachers are generally already more aligned in practice since they are smaller organisations with teachers fulfilling more similar roles, have *less* need for teacher alignment since teachers do not tend to 'share' pupils. They can function quite well even if each teacher invents their own behaviour policy, for example. Schools with a high degree of aligned practice often benefit novice teachers the most, who would otherwise struggle with choosing and establishing student routines. Where schools pursue alignment, they might think of it as a costly investment for experienced teachers that is gifted to the more novice ones. Jim Knight, a popular proponent of instructional coaching in the US, recognises this tension:

> *The directive approach to coaching also often fails because it over simplifies the rich, complex world of the classroom. ...What teachers and students need is an approach to coaching that combines the facilitative coach's respect for the professionalism of teachers with the directive coach's ability to identify and describe effective strategies that can help teachers move forward.*[155]

The expectation that an approach can resolve rather than work within innate complexity inevitably distorts it. The monitorial system could not produce homogenous learning outcomes in students. This was not a limitation of the model as such but a product of the dissonance between the model and expectations and regularities built into the school system. Instructional coaching, if it becomes the answer to the question, 'How do you ensure teaching consistency and quality?', could befall a similar fate. It could become untethered from important contextual and content considerations as it is reoriented towards the same alluring genericism and naïve expectations that characterise ill-fated solutions.

And in any case, before we abandon whole-staff professional development meetings, we should remember that practices persist because they serve functions, even if it is hard to see exactly what they are. The landscape of the classroom is largely hidden and highly complex. Schools and teachers develop rituals and routines that help them to navigate this terrain in a sustainable manner. Rituals help shape the story that staff tell themselves about their work and their professional identity, if not the work itself.[156] The collective confidence and shared sense of purpose that meetings can engender may help teachers make peace with the day-to-day ambiguity, uncertainty and impossibility of their individual jobs.

One day, Paula, Jane, Lucas or Asmitha might step up to lead these meetings, perhaps driven by a desire to influence events beyond their own classroom. It will be their turn to 'improve' their school. This will inevitably involve turning to their colleagues and advising them how to become a better teacher. It will be hard for them to avoid the same mistakes as those they once criticised. And it will be hard for them to deliver in this new role without feeling that these meetings have purpose. Do they forget what it feels like to be that teacher on a full timetable, or does the sheer diversity of classroom practice overwhelm them? It is to the minds and practices of these leaders that we turn in the next chapter.

Complex advice

Teachers are mostly left alone to get on with the job, with little meaningful engagement with other teachers. The surface-level similarity of classrooms hides a diversity of beliefs and practices. Any attempt to change teaching practice must acknowledge this isolation and diversity.

For those charged with changing the practice of teachers, we suggest the following:

1. Look beyond the surface-level similarity of teaching practice to understand the diverse beliefs and motivations of teachers.
2. Study teacher habits and incorporate the disruption and re-making of habits into professional development strategy.
3. Develop a dialogue with teachers about their adaptive responses to changing practice. Watch out for compliancy expertise and behaviour that is aimed at signalling compliance.
4. Consider what can be put in place to reduce professional isolation but be cautious in disrupting opportunities for teachers to recharge.
5. If you no longer teach a full timetable, remain conscious of the tension between expectation and reality that a whole day in the classroom invariably and repeatedly exposes.

Reflective questions

- Do the sketch descriptions of teachers in an after-school professional development session remind you of people you know? What other characters would you add to this story?
- In what ways are classrooms you have visited 'superficially similar'? From where do these similarities emerge?
- What insight do you have into where your beliefs as a teacher diverge from others you know or work with?
- To what extent does 'the avoidance of controversy' stifle school improvement discussions in your experience?
- What 'compliancy expertise' have you observed in schools? To what extent do teachers become experts in being observed, completing audits, filling in tracking spreadsheets or saying the right things to senior leaders?
- Do the professional development processes you have participated in or observed promote conformity or diversity?

CHAPTER 8 – YOU SHOULD DO THIS

*So, like savages before their gods, they worship facts.
And in return, the facts hit them like hailstones. Life
is just one damned fact after another. They turn
to collecting facts – laying them down – making
'Outlines' of every real and fancied fact in the universe,
until 'truth' becomes an endless succession of stepping-
stones that have a way of disappearing into the bog as
soon as they are passed over.*

Max Plowman, 1932[157]

The complexity of classrooms and of schools – a heady mix of
diverse motivations, beliefs, behaviour and understanding – cannot
be comprehended by a single mind. There is a necessity to simplify,
homogenise, if one is to make sense of school: to group the superficially
similar, to identify patterns and apparent causal links between events.

For those charged with influencing what transpires in a school, there is
a demand that they do something despite the complexity of the task. For
school leaders, this requires that they form a hypothesis about what it is
they are there to do and how their actions may affect what happens. This
'identity' shapes how school leaders act.[158] It is formed by their internal
dialogue, their dialogue with others and through their interaction with
their environment. From these interactions emerges a narrative about
school leadership that helps those in leadership positions make sense of
their role: how they interpret their experiences and thus how they set out
to control events.[159]

The question is whether the prevailing narratives, both public and private, which inform the identity of school leaders result in productive endeavours. School leaders readily instruct teachers to do things, but what drives the frequency and nature of these instructions?

To answer this, let us begin by considering the public narrative around school leadership that influences a leader's identity and how this in turn affects the instructions they give to teachers. We will argue that the expectation on school leaders is that they adopt an overly interventionist approach, particularly when it comes to what happens in the classroom, and that they are cast as 'fixers' of error and dysfunction. Furthermore, we will assert that it is the complex nature of schooling that, if not countenanced, leads to this problematic identity and, at worst, to significant efforts spent on attempting to solve illusory and transient problems.

What do we expect of school leaders?

In his first term as headteacher in a new school, Matthew recalls numerous encounters with parents who politely welcomed him to the school but would then take the opportunity to express their personal hopes for what perceived deficiencies he would be able to address on their behalf. Many of these involved a particular department that, to avoid any embarrassment to his colleagues, we will call the Basket Weaving Department. There was a great deal of dissatisfaction among many parents with the Basket Weaving Department that arose from anecdotal tales of what went on in lessons, told by their exasperated children when they arrived home from school, then shared at social events and through the newly burgeoning social media platforms. The profile of basket weaving at the school was made worse by generally disappointing exam results and instances of students who missed out on the grades they expected or were assured they would achieve. Matthew recalls feeling the weight of these remarks heavily as the reality of headship sunk in. This was now 'his problem'. Furthermore, in the eyes of these parents, he would now provide 'the solution'. He felt compelled to tell the Basket Weaving Department to do something – but what?

It is a commonly held view that headteachers should, first and foremost, directly influence what happens in the classroom. It is not only parents who hold this expectation; it is the underlying assumption of school improvement orthodoxy, leadership development programmes, successive Ofsted frameworks and even of teachers themselves who have been groomed to expect intervention to an extent that would have been unacceptable some decades ago. Given that the quality of teaching is now frequently cited as the most important influence on outcomes for pupils (above even 'leadership' in terms of its transformative power),[160] the desire by all those with a vested interest in school standards for some action to be taken to change what happens in classrooms is understandably strong. We need a solution therefore we must have one, and it is the headteacher, and the leaders who assist them in this task, who should provide it.

This expectation weighs heavy on the school leader because, having been a regular classroom teacher for some years before reaching these lofty heights, they have some insight into just how difficult the task before them will be. They can well remember the irresolvable dilemmas of the classroom that we described in chapter 3, which result from an attempt to meet the educational needs of a diverse population through a mass schooling system. Now that they are a headteacher standing some distance from the root problems, how should they solve these very same dilemmas that they themselves as teachers repeatedly failed to overcome?

The imposter syndrome felt by school leaders can be hard to shake: the nagging doubt as to whether they are any better placed as a third party to the process to influence positive change than they were when embedded in the daily life of the classroom. And yet, despite insight into the impossibility of the task, school leaders appear to take to offering advice and instructions to teachers readily. 'You Should Do This', they say. It is as if, once they cross the threshold between mere teacher and esteemed leader, they have privileged access to a pool of knowledge that enables them to see just what needs to happen in each classroom for improvement to take place. Where does this intervention urge arise from? If we had a unified approach to training school leaders, we may be less surprised by the consistency of their behaviour in this regard, but we do not. Are we simply appointing a certain type of people to leadership roles in schools (perhaps favouring those who think they have all the answers), or are there forces at work that drive leaders, whatever their background and disposition, to behave in similar ways?

We would argue that school leaders, as a group, are as diverse as the pool of teachers that they are drawn from.[161] They will have been influenced in their thinking about pedagogy by the disciplinary traditions of the subject they teach and the generation in which they were trained, which will in turn influence what they believe it is that other teachers should be doing. They will themselves have been on the receiving end of multiple 'You Should Do This' moments, which will inform their views on what is and is not helpful by way of intervention and instruction. Even their reasons for seeking a leadership position will vary, whether that be personal ambition, altruistic intent, the pursuit of power, higher income or a drive to achieve excellence. And of course, there is diversity of personality, which is so often cited as the source of a leader's style and modus operandi. It seems unlikely that homogeneity of behaviour can be attributed to a shared characteristic of such a diverse group.

School improvement discourses build an image of 'the leader' as an autonomous, powerful and omniscient presence and imagine them to be driving a school towards greater success. We take comfort in this narrative because the alternative, that headteachers and their senior teams cannot single-handedly do all that is asked of them, is too problematic to contemplate. While we can point to evidence that leadership at school level is a significant factor in the success of individual institutions,[162] is it not also the case that they are the product of, and are ultimately shaped by and constrained by, the system within which they operate?

Both the school itself, with its traditions, social norms, demographic constraints and institutional characteristics, and the wider educational system with its history, governance, power play and vested interests, serve to create and mould the form of school leadership that we may observe in schools. The apparent regularities hide a school system that is complex, diverse and evolving. Paradoxically, the system is both stable and unstable, and this tension is woven into the challenge for those charged with influencing what happens within it. We falsely attribute much of what we see the leader do to their strongly held values, inner strength (or weakness), personal characteristics and capability, rather than stepping back to view the leader as nested in a complex system that, if understood, might provide a better explanation for their actions. We are so interested in examining the influence of the leader we forget that they are also the subject of influence, not just by those in higher positions of authority, but more importantly by the system itself. How autonomous and powerful is the school leader in reality?

Just do something!

The orthodox view of leaders, promoted by pop-leadership literature and an army of consultants, is that they act decisively. It is better, it is argued, to be seen to take control and make decisions than to sit back and let events unfold. Leadership is, by definition, 'interventionist': the compulsion to influence, not to allow things just to happen. 'Laissez-faire' leadership is a defined style, but is talked about in derisory terms: what sort of leader would fail to rise to the challenge by allowing events to play out by themselves?

Of course, it is the job of those in a position of authority to influence what happens in a school. But how often should this influence be by instruction, and how readily do we expect school leaders to intervene directly to 'solve problems', particularly those that manifest in classrooms?

In Viviane Robinson's book *Reduce Change to Increase Improvement*, the author questions this tendency to *just do something*:

> *Why do we need to improve? What is wrong with what we are already doing? What exactly is the problem we are trying to solve? Without compelling answers to these questions, educators will not be committed to the hard work of improvement. Yet many leaders skip this stage of the improvement process, believing that such talk is negative and critical. Instead, they describe their wish to 'take advantage of an opportunity' or to adopt something they describe as 'best practice'. But frequently, such abstract and future-oriented rationales are only weakly motivating, for they fail to answer the inevitable comparative questions, such as why 'taking advantage of this opportunity' is better than not taking advantage of it. After all, there are an infinite number of 'opportunities for change', and most should probably not be taken.*[163]

Robinson describes the frequently observed habit of grasping at a solution without taking the time to understand the complexity of the problem – one that, she argues, leads to lots of change but not necessarily any improvement. She observes that most opportunities to do something different should not be taken: a call for caution, and possibly a decision not to act on the multitude of tempting 'good ideas'.

One of the reasons school leaders intervene is that action is valued over inaction because the outcome of doing something can be attributed to the actor, while the outcome of choosing to do nothing is not. The essayist Nassim Taleb points out that we recognise people for what they *did* do, not for what they *didn't* do, or avoided.[164] As Matthew has written elsewhere, 'Heroism is going into battle (whether we win or lose), not choosing to avoid the conflict. What remains unseen is the wise decision to delay whilst more information is gathered, the abandoned policy which would have wrought havoc, or the prevention of contradictory initiatives which overload those subject to them. Avoiding future disorder is an invisible act of strong leadership.'[165]

For evidence of this, compile your own list of initiatives that it would have been better if they had never happened. We might start with graded lesson observations, triple-impact marking, performance-related pay, three-part lessons, mini-plenaries, virtual learning platforms, interactive whiteboards, PeLTS (personal, learning and thinking skills) and most of the initiatives that came out of the pupil premium strategy. Might our schools be better places if these policy initiators had chosen to do nothing?

The compulsion to just do something is internalised psychologically by the school leader, but it arguably arises, or at least is encouraged and reinforced, externally to them. The initiatives above may only be plausible, or appear rational, in relation to a simplified model of the school, held in mind by those who attempt to comprehend it. This simulacrum, rather than a nuanced picture of a complex organisation, is endorsed and reinforced by the wider system. It is this abstraction that inspectors will access in their relatively brief and infrequent visits. Leaders experience pressure to curate an approved version of this imagined school and the expectation that the object of their interventions is primarily activities that take place in the classroom. Here we begin to see the systemic pressures that compel school leaders to, in turn, steer teachers with their good advice and non-negotiables.

The rejection of disorder

To fulfil the urge to do something, mechanisms are needed. In a complex system, this requires some order and for systems to be created, which is core to what we expect school leaders to do.

Schools are an attempt to create order. Their very existence suggests that young people's learning should not be haphazard or left to chance. This is the place where formal education happens. Children travel to this place in the morning and leave in the afternoon, slightly more 'schooled' than before. The school premises isolate children from chance encounters with the outside world: often a physical boundary – a semi-permeable membrane that filters unwanted entities. Once inside, they are channelled through corridors (without running!) to their designated rooms, where they will learn 'subjects' (ordered knowledge), according to a timetable, in groups that are deliberately constructed to reduce the complexity of the teaching task. Children of similar age or ability will be placed together to work towards mastering a common curriculum, which will be examined in an orderly exam hall, sat in rows, in silence, with no distractions allowed. Rules and routine mark out the most orderly schools. Punctuality is prized, attendance is awarded, shouting is sanctioned, silence is solicited.

The desire for order is ever present in schools, for example when schools seek to establish and re-establish 'good routines' after every holiday, between each lesson and within the classroom itself. While the psychological need to create order will vary between individuals,[166] there are systemic reasons why we find ourselves walking a line between order and disorder, and why we ask teachers to facilitate learning in particular ways. These observations are not made as a critique of schools. The 'factory model' criticism of schooling is a tired cliché. Enterprise requires order. Humans create similar structures wherever they are needed: shopping centres, festivals, workplaces, conferences. Excessive disorder is a barrier to endeavour.

The benefits of order are most apparent in the classroom. Opportunities for distraction must be minimised to allow attention to be paid to the curriculum object in question. Indeed, it has been suggested that the central purpose of schooling is to teach pupils to 'pay proper attention'.[167] But gaining attention is no mean feat: the teacher finds themselves in competition with multiple alternative interests and battling against a variety of emotional states. Each pupil brings a different past to the classroom and a different way of seeing the world. Even the words spoken by the teacher will have subtly different meanings and associations in the child's mind as they connect 'new learning' to their existing mental model, making sense of what they hear in unique ways. There is an 'unavoidable ambiguity' to the teaching of new concepts: a limitless opportunity for confusion and misconception. The skilful teacher will be mindful of the potential for disorder, distraction, disaffection and error, compensating with focus, precision and clarity. There is a never-ending quest for greater certainty and the elimination of irrelevance.

The degree of order that is desirable in a school is a dichotomous problem, and one for which there is no 'right' answer. An attempt to achieve higher levels of order within a school may be a response to conditions outside of the school: a more disordered social environment for children in the community meaning that greater stability and predictability are advantageous. The recent 'silent corridors' debate highlights how a degree of order deemed necessary in one school might appear abhorrent to those in less complex contexts. Similarly, order may be a response to greater spontaneity, for example the erratic behaviour of younger children in contrast to the more predictable behaviours of older students, who require fewer boundaries. The position taken may vary over time, as values and priorities change. The dynamic nature of our complex school system means that prevailing orthodoxies will rightly shift, often meaning pendulum-like swings between the order and chaos polarities. At times, and in certain contexts, greater disorder may be appealing. Disorder may have a moral appeal: placing liberty and individual freedoms over the needs of the organisation. Variety, spontaneity, individualism, discord, divergence and localism may all be prized, each one a pull towards the chaotic end of the spectrum.

'You Should Do This' moments are driven by the expectation that school leaders should do *something* about what happens in the classroom, but it is the order/disorder dichotomy that often underlies *what* it is teachers are asked to do:

- You should get better control of your class.
- You should think about the sequence of topics.
- You should explain this more clearly.
- You should monitor pupils' progress.
- You should have mini-plenaries throughout the lesson.
- You should create knowledge organisers.

Order is a form of simplification. If we can reduce complexity to a set of observable patterns, we might make sense of it, perhaps even hope to control it. It is the commonalities of the system that we seek to change to deliver our goals, not the differences. The diversity of teaching practices and classroom dynamics threatens to overwhelm us, so instead we seek to achieve consistency and look to influence the surface-level similarities.

The urge to align

Coupled with the urge for order is the urge to align. In chapter 7, we described the diversity of beliefs held by teachers and how these lead to a lack of conformity between what happens in one classroom, and the next. The surface features of a typical classroom design – one teacher, 30 children, desks in rows, teacher talking and asking students questions – are a superficial order that masks the underlying complexity of teaching practices. Rather than embracing this diversity, school leaders will often choose to inhibit it (or attempt to) through efforts to align how teachers practise their craft. This may be a wise decision as the unfettered whims of thousands of teachers seem unlikely to generate optimal conditions for learning. It would be hard to argue against some attempt to align beliefs and practices, but it is debatable how possible it is to achieve this to any great degree, at least without causing inadvertent harm. We have argued that efforts to promote greater consistency may, particularly where the pre-existing level of homogeneity is less than assumed, in fact lead to even more diversity as teachers interpret and adapt to new instructions in multiple and unpredictable ways. New information ricochets off teachers positioned at odds to one another.

Beyond these direct instructions to teachers, the urge to align can be observed in the vision statements, celebrated values and the strategic plans that are carefully crafted by school leaders and governing boards. Rhetoric alone is of course insufficient to achieve synergy of belief and action. Words pitched against complexity, the art of persuasion, will undoubtedly need the stronger arm of coercion if some degree of conformity is to be achieved. However, we should not be fooled into thinking that the stability and alignment we observe are necessarily a result of the leader's influence. Complex systems will generate patterns of behaviour that evolve over time. The astute leader may become skilful at observing the way the school is evolving and launch their initiative at the tipping point of change. In this way, the leader calls for the dog to come to him at the very moment he sees it is about to break into a run: the illusion of influence and control.

We should not assume that alignment is always preferable to diversity for pupils in our schools. For alignment read *boredom*, and for diversity read *variety*: the latter will undoubtedly be the preference of the child as they move between classes. Diversity is experimentation, the dipping of the toe in the water. Diversity of perspectives builds a more comprehensive description of the problem at hand, or a critical engagement with the proposed solution. When we celebrate the benefits of conformity, we should also weigh up the opportunity cost of greater diversity.

We might see the urge to align, like the desire for order, as a psychological feature of the leader. However, it is the extent of diversity in schools that makes this urge so strong. Separating the leader from the system will mean we have a narrow view of what is happening, whereas situating the leader as part of the system allows us to see their actions not only as attributable to their personal values and beliefs, but as an inevitable consequence of the complexity of the schools they operate within.

Seeking to impose order and alignment inevitably involves some complexity denial as one goal, purpose or perspective is focused on at the expense of others. Leaders will feel push-back from these efforts as conflicts emerge with other values and desires. The more they pursue an agenda, the more resistance they will feel, and there is a pressure to row back on initiatives. The urge to 'just do something' becomes a feeling that they should 'just do something else'. Thereby, 'You Should Do This' becomes 'you should do this instead'. This, as we shall see in chapter 9, creates wave upon wave of school policies and interventions that may be labelled as management ineffectiveness, but that might more constructively be seen as the almost inevitable consequence of complexity denial. How do we break this cycle?

Shadow boxing

If we frame leaders as autonomous agents who may, due to individual variations in efficacy, execute the role particularly well or particularly badly then we fail to consider the role of the wider system in shaping behaviours. As Seymour B. Sarason observes, 'Unless one deals with "the system" – unless one's efforts involve changing system characteristics – it is unlikely that we will be more than shadow boxing with the real problems.'[169]

The school leader as 'shadow boxer', punching away at illusory or transient problems, is not a metaphor you see espoused often in the management literature. In the quote above, Sarason is not suggesting that the leader is without influence but rather that it is wise to question the external, as well as internal, source of their intent – to acknowledge the wider context within which they decide to act. If we are not careful, school leaders become mere shadow boxers: their punches are strong, but they continuously fail to land any knockout blows.

What is it about the wider system that promotes shadow boxing? Perhaps the answer lies to some extent in the prevailing views about how we go about improving schools. If the conventional wisdom is to be believed, we do it by tackling one deficiency at a time, by closing one gap at a time, by implementing one intervention at a time. We train new school leaders to behave this way. We present a pick-and-mix of evidence-informed solutions that leaders are encouraged to import into their schools. We frame the problems facing education in terms of 'gaps' and 'deficiencies'. If we view school leaders in this way – as fixers – their life (to paraphrase Plowman's quote at the start of this chapter) will become just one damned fix after another, and school improvement 'an endless succession of stepping-stones that have a way of disappearing into the bog as soon as they are passed over'. To the teacher, this tendency presents as a series of initiatives or instructions intended to 'fix' classroom problems – try this, now try this, now this…

Creeping managerialism

When you go behind the label 'human error', you see people and organisations trying to cope with complexity, continually adapting, evolving along with the changing nature of risk in their operations.

D. Woods, *Behind Human Error*[170]

When school leaders start looking for problems, they usually find them. They are particularly astute at spotting where people make mistakes. In complex systems, mistakes are normal and will often arise because human beings working in such an environment are overwhelmed in some way: by the amount of work to be done, the number of directives to follow, the moral ambiguity of the dilemmas they face or in trying to keep up with the ever-changing list of policies they are expected to comply with. Errors are particularly irritating to leaders if they occur in a system that they feel they have carefully designed and implemented. They take these errors either as a sign that they were not clear enough about how this new initiative should be enacted, or that those subject to them are incompetent. Either way, they will be really irked by the mistakes. The tendency to attribute errors to people rather than to the system in which those people operate is common.

Rather than look towards complexity for the cause of error, it is more often the case that school leaders will directly address the error-maker and apply a 'patch' to the problem. Patches may come in the following forms:

- a clarification as to what the error-maker should have done
- a chastisement for not following the prescribed rules
- a wider clarification of protocol to ensure others do not make the same mistake
- an additional diktat (flow diagram, detailed guidance, new rules) that assume that the error was due to a lack of clarity and precision, or a minor design flaw
- increased monitoring to ensure the problem is not more widespread
- additional training
- pressure to ensure that there is compliance with the rules of the initiative

These patches are all 'corrective' in that they assume that the error need not have happened and only a minor adjustment is needed to get the intervention back on track. We came across this phenomenon in chapter 3, where the classroom teacher is engaged in similar patch-making behaviour when faced with the inevitable gaps in pupils' knowledge. We all, teachers, leaders and policymakers, make these attribution errors when faced with complex situations that are neither entirely within our control nor that of any other individual agent. This is not to say that individuals are always without fault, but by failing to look beyond that fault we limit our insight into the error.

When multiple or serious errors occur, it is tempting to continue to apply patches and step up the pressure on those making the mistakes. Over time, this tendency leads to a creeping managerialism whereby the school is overloaded with prescriptive policies, excessive monitoring and high levels of psychological pressure to perform. The irony of this is that the environment will become even more complex for people to navigate, which leads to an increase in the frequency and seriousness of mistakes. Had the leader recognised error as a sign of excessive complexity and sought to address this by making it simpler and easier for teachers to make decisions, this managerial spiral would have been avoided. Instead, the application of endless patches adds complexity on top of complexity, making error increasingly likely.

A complex system, contrary to what people believe, does not require complicated systems and regulations and intricate policies. The simpler, the better. Complications lead to multiplicative chains of unintended consequences, followed by apologies about the 'unforeseen' aspect of the consequences, then to another intervention to correct secondary effects, leading to an explosive series of branding 'unforeseen' responses, each one worse than the preceding one.

Nassim Nicholas Taleb, *Antifragile*[171]

To the complexity-denier, error is a signal that leadership needs to be 'stronger'. This is a problem they believe can be corrected through further instruction, more detailed guidance, more forceful coercion and more attentive monitoring. The 'fix it' mentality arises from seeing the system as complicated rather than complex. In a complicated system, we are correct to think of a malfunctioning system as 'broken'. A deterministic system is either working or not working, and if the latter then it needs to be fixed. However, such binary thinking is unhelpful in relation to a complex system that always runs in degraded mode. We cannot simply remove the faulty part and replace it because the 'fault' does not reside as a component in isolation, but rather is the consequence of a complex dynamic that we may or may not fully understand. Behaving as if the system is merely complicated by applying 'one damned fix after another' will lead to unintended consequences and potentially damaging interventions. Not only is the 'fix' harmful, but it may also disrupt something that helped the system operate well in other ways (as we discuss in chapter 9).

Of course, school leaders will be taken in by the illusions described above to different extents. We contend that leaders who develop an awareness of the true complexity of the school system are less likely to find themselves shadow boxing with an imagined version of the school.

Whether it is friendly advice, managerial correction or the Next Big Thing, the tendency to intervene in what happens in the classroom is shaped by the system's complexity. So too is the nature and scope of these instructions. We expect our school leaders to repeatedly attempt to solve the fundamental problems of schooling: to do something – anything! – to bring about change. And if the object of our attention cannot be fully comprehended then it must be brought under control, simplified and homogenised, so that we can at least influence the surface features of the system. Everyone expects school leaders to do this and will take comfort that it is attempted, regardless of whether they succeed.

None of this would be a problem if the things we asked teachers to do were always helpful. As we shall see in the next chapter, when teachers are told 'You Should Do This', perhaps they really shouldn't. The urge to intervene and fix is strong but can be excessive and harmful if it goes unchecked.

Complex advice

To help school leaders take a measured view of their role we suggest the following:

1. Recognise and celebrate decisions *not* to act when caution and delay are prudent.
2. Critically evaluate 'good ideas', not just on their own merit but in relation to the plethora of other good ideas that could be acted upon. Why this one? What problem does it solve?
3. Confront the urge to create order and alignment and question your motives for this. Will this enable a more productive environment or merely satisfy your need to understand and control?
4. To what extent are your interventions determined by what gaps and deficiencies you notice and that irk you? Question your tendency to attribute error to a quality of an individual or group rather than as an inevitable consequence of pursuing a complex endeavour.
5. Watch out for corrective, patch-making behaviour and correct for this by considering the complex causes of the organisational behaviours that concern you.

Reflective questions

- To what extent does your school (or a school you know of) value order and alignment? What is it about the school's context that affects how much order/consistency or disorder/diversity it tolerates?
- What 'You Should Do This' moments have you witnessed (or perhaps been subject to)? Was this issued as friendly advice, as corrective, or due to someone's 'good idea'?
- How often is the advice offered to teachers, in your opinion, helpful?
- To what extent do you recognise description of school leaders as 'fixers' who tackle 'one deficiency at a time'? Do you know of school leaders who appear to avoid this trap? What do they do (or not do) that is different?

CHAPTER 9 – NAÏVE INTERVENTION

> *Here is Edward Bear, coming downstairs now, bump, bump, bump, on the back of his head, behind Christopher Robin. It is, as far as he knows, the only way of coming downstairs, but sometimes he feels that there really is another way, if only he could stop bumping for a moment and think of it.*
>
> A. A. Milne, Winnie-the-Pooh[172]

It is fair to say that headteachers are a committed and well-intentioned bunch of people: certainly, the vast majority of those we have met are. They work hard for their communities and are often driven by a strong moral purpose. Given the inherent challenges of running a school day to day, let alone the difficulty of improving the quality of education in a school over time, most in the profession would not choose to swap places with their headteacher.

And yet, headteachers (and their senior teams) can make decisions that appear questionable – even plain daft. They launch initiatives that falter, make pronouncements they will later contradict, appear to act in ways that go against their espoused beliefs and get in the way of teachers trying to get on with their jobs. Even those who avoid such mistakes will, on occasion, pursue school improvement strategies that never really deliver sustainable and meaningful change. There are some notable schools that have been transformed thanks (allegedly) to a leader's clear sight and determination, but these are exceptions. Most seem to just get by, doing a pretty good job of educating children, improving some specific aspects of their provision, while standards slip elsewhere.

It is difficult to support the above claims with contemporary examples because what we subscribe to now seems eminently reasonable and justified, as we illustrated in relation to the curriculum wave in chapter 6. Many of the current set of accepted practices are rational given the prevailing orthodoxy of our time. However, ask a long-standing school leader about their past school improvement efforts and they will cringe at some of the things they publicly endorsed: the time spent embedding cross-curricular skills in subjects, training teachers to use 'thinking hats', helping children build 'learning power' or promoting three-part lessons. When we look back in years to come on our current preoccupations, how misguided will we appear to our future selves?

In this chapter, we will discuss leadership mishap and misadventure that occurs when leaders are in denial of the complexity of their school and the wider system. There is a risk that we over-emphasise error and under-appreciate the important work that school leaders do. This is not our intention. Instead, by analysing where and why leadership can go awry, we hope to create a greater awareness of the traps of unknowledge and complexity so that we may better avoid them in the future. We do so with great respect and affection for school leaders as they take on the impossible task of overcoming the fundamental problems of schooling.

There are many possible reasons why school leaders make unwise decisions and take counter-productive or ineffective action. We might attribute this to some characteristic of the individual: incompetence, ill-intent or ethical shortfall. But if we look beyond individual error and explore the systemic factors that create the operational conditions for school leaders, we may better understand why missteps are so widespread.

Three factors may help explain many of the questionable behaviours exhibited by some school leaders, all of which we have discussed in earlier chapters, but that we will bring together here to explain the phenomena of leadership mishap. First, we have significant gaps in our knowledge about schools and the school system that create an intellectual vacuum around school improvement. Second, school leaders are compelled to fill this vacuum with unproven innovations and 'fixes' to the problems they perceive. Finally, they may do so without fully comprehending the diverse and complex reality of their schools, the emergent behaviours of the system or the importance of the regularities they seek to replace. We term this phenomenon 'complexity denial'.

Put more crudely, school leaders often do not really know enough to make informed decisions but feel a strong sense that they must do *something* (as we discussed in chapter 8), so may adopt ideas that fail to take account of the characteristics of the system they are acting upon. They are propelled to act naïvely, blindly, but with the passioned intent to make things better for the children in their care. It is by no means inevitable that leadership plays out in this way, and yet it often does.

How do leaders know what to do?

Tasked with the job of improving a school, where does a school leader turn for inspiration? They may look to import strategies that appear to have worked elsewhere, perhaps in the previous school in which they worked, from a high-performing school nearby or from the Education Endowment Foundation's menu of 'proven' interventions. Alternatively, they may look inwards and develop approaches to incrementally address perceived weaknesses in the school. These two strategies – copying and innovating – are used across industries with great success. However, in education both are fraught with difficulties.

To understand these improvement strategies better, let's draw on an analogy provided by the economist Tim Harford in his book *Messy*.[173] Harford asks us to imagine that we enter a competition to find the highest point (grid reference) on the planet, without being allowed to look at a map. We are against the clock. Each time we pick a grid reference, we are told its altitude above sea level. What is our best strategy?

It is unlikely that we will win by either picking random grid references or by working methodically through them. One alternative is that we use a 'hill climbing' strategy whereby we choose a grid reference at random, then pick points around this to see which is higher, continuing this process until every proximate point is downhill. At this point we know we have reached a 'local summit'. However, this summit is more likely to be a small hill than a tall mountain.

Harford explains that the most likely winning approach will combine randomness and hill-climbing. This strategy would have you pick a variety of random points for a while as you look for signs of where the mountain ranges appear to be. As time moves on, you select the highest point you have hit so far and randomly select points within a few kilometres to test out where the highest peaks in the range might be. Finally, in the dying minutes of the competition, you should settle on the highest point found and start hill-climbing until you reach the peak.

The lesson of this analogy is that pure 'hill climbing' strategies will only enable us to peak the nearest summit. Sometimes we need to go beyond our current territory and look for a higher peak. Unlike in this fictional competition, we need not randomly pick schools to find this higher ground: we have maps that tell us where to look, although these maps are produced by researchers rather than Ordnance Survey. However, as we discussed in chapter 2, these maps are far from being dependable sources of information about 'what works'. Therefore, our search for higher terrain is not random, but neither is it entirely informed. Furthermore, copying the ideas we come across into our school is fraught with difficulties.

The limitations of copying

Many industries successfully harness copying to drive economic growth. One company hits on a good idea and the other companies are able to copy them, thus improving the service for all customers. This model *should* work out well in our largely collaborative rather than competitive industry, where school leaders who believe they are on high ground are generally very happy to share intelligence. However, while it seems instructive that we should encourage school leaders to copy good practice in other schools, in reality the process of identifying and transplanting effective practices is fraught with difficulties.

Imagine a primary school that, on the face of it, seems to have improved its reading test scores. You contact said school and the headteacher agrees that reading is now vastly better taught than before. They tell you this is thanks to the implementation of the Lorem Ipsum Reading programme and suggest that you purchase it, too. It may indeed improve your school too, but only providing that each of the following holds:

1. Reading at *their* school is indeed better, rather than the school having improved their SATs preparation, their intake demographic or simply got lucky one year on tests.[174]
2. Their implementation of the Lorem Ipsum Reading programme is indeed the key mechanism by which they improved reading instruction at their school. (School leaders will inevitably develop neat narratives as to the causes of their success.)[175]
3. The difficulties with reading in your own school are well-aligned with theirs, so that Lorem Ipsum Reading can, in principle, fix problems you have in the same way it might have done for them.
4. You can purchase the programme and implement it in the same, exact manner within your own school.

If any individual condition is violated, then the mechanism of copying that is so successfully applied in other industries will tend to fail in our own. The invisibility of learning and complexity both serve to hinder the chances that all these conditions can hold. It is no wonder that strategies brought into a school by leaders who have seen them work elsewhere will often fail to have the same effect.

Given that both copying and using ideas from the 'what works' map are both fraught with difficulties, leaders may be forgiven for becoming inward looking; getting their heads down and climbing the hill they are on.

Hill climbing

If they are not looking outwards for good ideas to copy, school leaders will look to self-innovate solutions for the problems that manifest in their own school. However, they are not insulated from the wider system and therefore the problems they notice, the way they perceive these problems and the nature of the solutions they innovate will be influenced by forces outside of their control.

We suggest six systemic problems that may beset school leaders who adopt hill climbing strategies:

- **The identity problem.** A school leader's identity is influenced strongly by external factors that they may or may not be aware of but will be adaptive to (as we described in chapter 8).

- **The patch-making tendency.** School leaders tend to attribute error to individuals and groups rather than understanding the wider systemic forces that lead to human behaviours and as a result are prone to apply 'patches' to problems (also described in chapter 8).
- **The emergence of myths.** School leaders will be influenced by the accepted wisdom of the time and by the myths that emerge to fill the gaps in our collective knowledge about how to improve schools.
- **The imagined school problem.** School leaders form an 'imagined school' in mind, which is by necessity a simplified and partial representation of the true complexity of the school. This imagined school is the basis for their decision making and can become the object of their influence, rather than the school itself.
- **The positional problem.** School leaders' perceptions are subjective and determined by how they are positioned in relation to the problems they attempt to solve. What seems like an 'obvious' solution to them may not appear so to others.
- **The disruption of regularities.** School leaders may underestimate the importance of the regularities of behaviour (the train tracks along which the school runs) and implement innovations that disrupt functionality.

These six problems are functions of a wider issue that is the individual leader's blind spot regarding the true complexity of the system within which they work. Nassim Taleb[176] describes the iatrogenic effects of leaders in denial of complexity: that is, the harmful unintended consequences caused while trying to be helpful. He terms these harmful actions *naïve interventions*. Naïve interventions arise because we believe the system is simpler, more predictable and more controllable than it truly is. Again, we should note that we are not arguing that anyone in a position of influence in the education system is ill-intentioned, stupid or wilfully negligent; rather that complexity largely goes unacknowledged and therefore harmful unintended consequences are common. Furthermore, there exist feedback loops that work against school leaders becoming aware of their naïvety, as we shall see later in this chapter.

We discussed two of the above problems in chapter 8, so let us now examine the others in more detail.

The emergence of myths

In chapters 1 and 2, we highlighted the domains of 'unknowledge' that make it so difficult for those acting upon the system to achieve positive, significant and sustainable change. School leaders operate within an intellectual vacuum whereby it is incredibly difficult to identify, replicate and scale-up allegedly effective approaches, and to learn whether an intervention has achieved the intended effect.

This vacuum of understanding invites us to fill it. And fill it we do, often with ill-conceived innovations, truthy sentiments, unjustified claims, attractive narratives, superficial explanations and simplistic assertions. Education is a breeding ground for myths and positions taken with religious zeal. Attempts to rise above common myth making lay claim to scientific evidence to support their assertions. In the *ResearchED Guide to Education Myths*[177] we are warned about the myth that technology will solve the lock-step problem, that differentiation will enable personalised education within every classroom and that blocking the curriculum will help pupils focus on one topic at a time. These myths, it is argued, have been dispelled by the evidence of cognitive science. Guy Claxton, a target for the accusations of unfounded educational myths, retaliates against the neo-traditionalist's claim to the intellectual high ground by setting out his own set of myths that include the myth that memorisation frees up working memory, that facts must be taught before pupils can think and discuss and that developing skills is in competition with knowledge.[178] The claims of each side are made with reference to evidence, but rest more on metaphor than either party may like to admit. We cannot observe learning at a molecular level; therefore, we rely on metaphors and models that stop short of providing a mechanical description of how to improve learning (more on these myths later in this chapter).

Which of the myth-busters is right? This may not be a useful question as correctness is not the criteria against which ideas become accepted; rather they are given transient credibility by coalitions of advocates. The most popular ideas, those validated by successful schools and key players in the wider educational system, are the myths we are most likely to reach for. Perhaps we are drawn to believe compelling new narratives, or perhaps we are drawn to those that provide a legitimacy to our own school improvement efforts. Either way, the accuracy of each claim is not the basis for its legitimacy, although its proponents might believe it to be. The trouble is that the topography of success is regularly reformed as the plausibility of explanations wax and wane.

The problem with our unknowledge and myth making is that, to make the education system gradually more productive, we rely on school and system leaders developing expertise. But expertise in what? School leaders may indeed become more knowledgeable about their school but developing expertise in the craft of improving schools is far more challenging as we have no agreed framework or reliable model for doing so. Rather than coming to understand the dynamics of the education system better, leaders can be distracted by developing knowledge in the latest fad or policy initiative. During the data wave (described in chapter 5), many school leaders developed skills in creating pivot tables in a spreadsheet, designing lesson observation rubrics that described the progress pupils were making in a lesson, and supported subject leaders in creating assessment systems that generated numbers and grades to populate colourful tracking systems. This expertise was valued highly at the time and some senior leaders were appointed for their skills in data manipulation, but as the wave broke, many leaders were left bewildered at the lack of spreadsheet work there was left to do. The development of transient skills and of knowledge with a use-by date does not make for an efficient system or fulfilling work environment.

These practices are now decried as myths by Ofsted themselves.[179] At the end of the data wave, Ofsted started to push back against the dubious data sheets and excessive workload that many schools felt compelled to engage in. Such rational argument against these practices implicitly places responsibility for their emergence upon the misinterpretations or statistical illiteracy of school leaders. However, during peak data, great big spreadsheets *were* an integral element of the stories that school leaders were compelled to tell. For a time, the presence of these mythical solutions provided schools with the legitimacy (and Ofsted grading) that allowed them to carry on with their work. As we explored in chapter 6, the wider narrative has shifted; legitimacy is now to be found in curriculum artefacts, processes and practices. New myths and metaphors.

New myths are the concepts and models that, via an emergent process of reification, gain transient solidity. These are the building blocks that leaders are most likely to reach for when constructing their schools. Like the wisest of the three pigs, they believe these concepts to be solid stone, where in fact they are ice-bricks, which will melt away in time.

What is the edifice school leaders set out to build? An edifice is defined as both a large, imposing building and as a complex system of beliefs. School leaders hold in mind an edifice in this latter sense: a mental image of what they believe their school *is* and *should be*.

The imagined school

School leadership is an act of imagination. School leaders must imagine the school, the entity they are acting upon, to be something, and imagine what it might one day become. But how does the school leader imagine their school to be?

To function in their roles, school leaders must create their own explanatory mental model of the school upon which they act, although this model will be necessarily partial. As we noted in chapter 6, Keil suggests that humans construct a model of their environment that preferences the features that are more easily seen or visualised; 'thus, the more easily visible are parts in a system, relative to hidden ones, the stronger the illusion of explanatory depth'. Given the unknowledge that marks our understanding of education, and the vast complexity and diversity of schools, an individual's conception of education will be flawed, but we will have 'a compelling sense of knowing more than we do'.[181]

An example of this illusion is the school leaders' perceptions of the daily experiences of pupils and teachers in classrooms. The surface features of classroom activity, visible to them as they walk the corridors and observe lessons, create a sense of 'knowing' what is going on across the school. They may satisfy themselves that classes are calm, that pupils are productive and that teachers are controlling behaviour. However, the hidden – and arguably more important – features of the classroom, such as the subtle social dynamics, thoughts and feelings of the pupils and intentions and motivations of the teachers remain unknown to them. There is also a tendency to homogenise 'the class' and codify the activity within it to enable managerial judgements and comparisons to be made. Insights into the lives of learners and teachers are inferred through abstraction and preference the visible. This may provide the school leader with an exaggerated feeling of knowing.

School leaders must also imagine how the things they observe came to be. In doing so, it is expedient for them to assume simple causal explanations. The children's poem *For Want of a Nail* is a good example of such an explanation. It paints a vivid picture of how a missing 'horseshoe nail' eventually leads to the fall of an entire kingdom.[182] This form of explanation is appealing but rarely mirrors the real world as multiple feedback loops cause events to unfold in spontaneous and unpredictable ways with many interlinked causal factors at play. As Nancy Cartwright observed: causes work in teams.[183]

The imagined school – the necessarily simplistic model of reality that the school leader holds in mind – is the reference point for a leader's decisions. When they ask a teacher to 'do this', we may assume their instructions are rational in relation to this model. What we do not know is how well this construct reflects the true reality of the school.

Tragically, the school leader's attempts to understand the complexity of their school can create an imagined school that is some distance from reality. Unable to witness or comprehend the events which play out in classrooms across the school, they will invent proxies that provide the information upon which they create their imagined school. These proxies – the data points, observation evidence, flight paths, curriculum maps – may *become* the school in the mind of the leader: the thing upon which they act. Where this illusion takes hold, leaders' instructions may target the proxy measures rather than tangible experiences of those within the community. Teachers may be asked to 'turn the reds into greens' on the spreadsheet, teach more 'outstanding' lessons, achieve positive value-added with their class or ensure there is a retrieval task at the start of each lesson. 'You Should Do This' moments become surreal instructions, divorced from the teachers' and pupils' true experience of learning. Yet the school leader may be pure in their intent, convinced of their rightness and entirely rational in their decision making. They are genuinely surprised when their 'knockout blows' make no connection, thrown off balance by the momentum of their conviction. Perhaps, as we suggest in chapter 8, they find themselves only shadow boxing with real problems.

In this abstracted institution, idealistic aims can be mistaken for mechanical explanations. Gaps can be closed; mindsets can be changed; exceptional progress can be made despite the absence of any blueprints containing credible explanations for how to consistently realise these ends. The imagined school is the frame of reference for decision making and, at worst, can also become the object upon which the leader exercises their influence, rather than the school itself.

Perspective

The way we see the world is determined by our past experiences, which in turn form our frames of reference. In familiar, non-complex, situations our myopic sense-making may not be problematic but in schools we often need to draw on a wider range of viewpoints to even begin to understand what is going on. As Beck and Plowman put it: 'for rare and unusual events that bring confusion and ambiguity, bringing conflicting perceptions to the surface can help the organisation hear from a broad set of voices and minimise the chance of acting precipitously'.[184]

The trouble occurs when school leaders are in denial of complexity and thus do not recognise the need to seek out alternative perspectives to comprehend situations more fully. Their interpretation of events makes sense *to them*, and they can probably quickly identify an 'obvious' solution that falls logically out of the way the problem is perceived. This is an example of Maslow's Law of the Instrument, which we introduced in chapter 6.[185] If you only have a hammer, you will see everything as a nail. If your job title is 'data manager' then you will pay attention to the data: problems will manifest through the prism of data analysis and solutions will be attractive if data might play a significant role. Similarly, pastoral leaders will define problems as being caused by pastoral deficits and seek to identify pastoral solutions. This bias is alluring as interpreting our environment in subjective ways gives our role meaning. It makes us powerful leaders able to deliver the improvements required by our performance management targets.

It is the perspective of school leaders that often dominates how problems within schools are defined, and that get paid any attention. Leaders imagine that the 'helicopter view' they possess privileges their insights, enabling them to pinpoint what is 'going wrong'. The dominance of leader perspectives in the choice of school improvement strategies is problematic as leaders are influenced by where they look and how they perceive what they see. If they choose to spend time observing lessons, then inevitably they will identify the cause of the school's problems as arising from the deficits in practice they believe they have observed. If they are present around the school at lesson changeover times and at breaks, they will more likely notice unruly behaviour that appears to be left unchallenged as other staff are not present to address it. The solution falls out easily from the problem definition – require teachers to step outside their classrooms to monitor behaviour. This is the breeding ground for managerialism: leaders' school improvement strategies that arise 'obviously' from their analysis, which in turn is informed by where they choose to look and how they are destined to perceive what they see.

Not only may school leaders be naïve about the various perspectives from which we can comprehend a complex problem, but also about the very nature of such problems. As noted in chapters 4 and 5, complex problems are metamorphic in that they re-emerge in new forms over time and at various levels within the system. Leaders will act naïvely if they believe that there is a perfect solution to the problem, or a 'right' way of proceeding. If a school leader is not attuned to the unintended consequences of their previous interventions, and how the features of the last 'solution' manifest in the latest problems, they will continue in their ignorance that they are as much a part of the current problem as they are a part of the next solution.

In denial of complexity, those charged with improving schools will do so without questioning their subjective perspective or simplistic view of the problems they face. Is it any wonder their well-meaning interventions have harmful effects? As we noted in chapter 8, they may often be better doing nothing. Instead, they try to 'fix' what they perceive is going wrong.

The importance of regularities

In their attempts to change things for the better, school leaders may not stop to think about why things are the way they are. In chapter 1, we explained the importance of regularities in schools and how they help the system function. Regularities are the habits and routines that define a school's daily operations – the train tracks along which they run. There is often no institutional memory of the origin and rationale for these regularities, and they may remain unquestioned for years. They are none the less vitally important as they enable those within the system to simplify the complex challenges they face and to steer the organisation away from chaotic behaviour.

The problem with introducing change into a school is that it will inevitably disrupt regularities and these regularities may perform a valuable, even vital, function. To intervene without taking the time to appreciate how a novel action may affect existing regularities is reckless, but it happens a great deal in schools. For an individual teacher, the regularities they have established within their own classrooms may or may not be optimal, but they will provide stability and security for both the teacher and the children in her classes. By imposing ill-considered change on the teacher, the school leader risks undermining structures and routines that perform an important function, even if that function is to give the teacher a reasonably predictable working day and enable them to find the mental space to address the matters that need their attention.

Under-appreciating regularities is another facet of complexity denial. Alongside the failure to seek out alternative perspectives to one's own and the tendency to attribute errors to individuals rather than looking for the reasons for these errors, riding roughshod over regularities is another ingredient in a potent brew of naïve interventionism.

The waltz

We might wonder how school leaders remain for so long in this state of complexity denial. Surely the teachers subject to their ill-considered actions will point out the error of their ways. As with the frictional encounter of the policy wave as it brushes up against the real school, which we highlighted in chapter 6, so too must the naïve intervention of school leaders encounter the reality of the classroom.

In a well-functioning system, those implementing ineffective interventions should receive feedback to indicate that the intended effect has not been achieved. However, effective feedback loops do not always exist, or may operate with long time-lags between leadership interventions and learning outcomes. As a result, decisions may have a 'bounded rationality' in that the immediate effects appear positive but, without full view of the extended impact of their actions, school leaders will remain ignorant about the cumulative effects.[186] The noisiness and delay of any signals indicating impact mean that, in the short and medium term, it is entirely rational for school leaders to pursue their strategies. It takes a long time for clear signals to cut through.

Feedback loops often fail because teachers choose not to voice their concerns if the instruction to 'do this' makes little sense to those at the chalkface. Sometimes they do, but this information may be taken as 'resistance to change' or the protestations of those not in possession of the privileged information of leaders. However, often those subject to reform will remain silent. How might we interpret this silence?

In chapter 7, we discussed the adaptive responses of teachers as they struggle to cope with the complexity and demand of their jobs. Confronted with confusing, unreasonable or nonsensical managerial demands, teachers may adopt strategies to avoid attention, such as passivity in professional development sessions, or signal compliance through the production of the required documentation or delivering the desired pedagogical techniques in show-lessons. These teachers just want to be left alone to get on with the job and it is in their interests to keep leaders 'busy', which means reinforcing the idea that what they are doing is meaningful. Consciously or subconsciously, teachers develop, and often successfully deploy, their compliancy expertise.

Alternatively, those teachers who are more sympathetic to the plight of school leaders to improve the school may wish to be supportive by superficially playing along with new initiatives, believing they are being kind by signalling to leaders that their efforts and ideas are worthwhile.

It is also possible that teachers believe that school leaders must know what they are doing, else why would they be school leaders? These teachers are complicit in complexity denial, assuming that the system is more known, more predictable and more controllable than is really the case. It is perhaps this last group who reinforce the complexity denial of leaders the most as they willingly implement the latest directive and make positive noises about novelty, assuming in their isolation that if it is not working for them then it must be their fault; that is, they must not be doing it right.

In such ways, leaders and teachers waltz together, moving around the dance floor but never really getting anywhere. Each is coping with a complex reality by maintaining the façade that improving education is quite straightforward. We may observe a variety of dances in schools: the observation dance, the data dance, the line management dance, the self-evaluation dance. These may be elegant and fluid, perfected by both partners. When leaders and teachers become caught up in the waltz it is easy to lose sight of whether anything of substance improves for the children in the school.

School leaders dance with the system too, and with the policy waves and accountability methods that they are subject to. Mostly, they want to be left alone to run their schools in the way they see fit, but they recognise that this is not possible. They will develop expertise in running a school but also work to master the school improvement dance that happens in the imaginary ballroom of politicians, bureaucrats, regulators and policymakers.

It is a bit more complex than that

Inevitably, the picture we have painted to explain why school leaders pursue unproductive improvement strategies will not capture the true complexity of what is going on. The systemic forces that influence the behaviour of school leaders constantly evolve and each leader, in each school context, will be affected in subtly different ways. However, it is our contention that our efforts to improve schools will be less harmful if those in positions of influence gain insight into the complex system dynamics that feed their identity, compel them to act and reduce their ability to do so wisely. Everyone involved in education wants to improve our schools, but the strength of our conviction is not enough.

The Next Big Thing is often ushered in on the strength of a narrative that privileges individual school leaders' capacity to transform their schools while simultaneously deriding their predecessors' efforts. The popularity of this assumption with leaders and policymakers is understandable. It would make their professional lives considerably easier were it true. It is misleading to cast the dynamic driving the widespread adoption of past trends as substantially different to that propelling the latest. Nevertheless, doing so allows leaders to conclude that their predecessors have done unwise things before proceeding to act in ways that their successors are likely to view with similar dubiety. The cult of the Next Big Thing is perennially reincarnated.

School leaders around the country as the data wave emerged may have individually engaged in a process of reflection, perhaps consultation with the EEF and leaders in similar schools, before carefully selecting a data management system and joining PiXL. This may have brought legitimacy to their institutions, and may, through the means of cultivating a shared myth around tackling disadvantage, have positively impacted upon direction and morale. However, these leaders work within as well as upon the complex education system. In this context decision making is shaped by bounded rationality (unknowledge even). To cast it as an individual rational, evidence-based decision was untrue at the time (when it was deemed the right thing to do by many) and is untrue now (where it is generally deemed a wrong-turn into a statistically illiterate cul-de-sac).

If we are to place so much responsibility for delivering a better education system on the shoulders of schools, we must be clear exactly what we expect school leaders to do. We need a school improvement methodology that is fit for purpose: one that acknowledges and equips school leaders for informed action in the face of complexity. We do not need one that, by over-simplifying the challenge of school improvement and exaggerating what it is possible to know, encourages a career of accepting, endorsing, recanting and replacing a succession of Next Big Things.

Not all school leadership is characterised by mishap and fad. There are many good things that school leaders do that make a difference and that last. When schools focus on making things better for children in tangible ways, in domains that are known, with goals that are clearly defined, and where proven transmission mechanisms exist, schools do indeed improve. However, where school leaders venture beyond the concrete and known, they must be careful to not let their imaginations run away with them. We are all story tellers, but our responsibility is to create narratives that move us forward. It is time to tell a more plausible story about school improvement.

Complex advice

The actions of school leaders will likely be rational given their frame of reference but may not always appear so to others. This is a consequence of a necessarily reductionist 'imagined school'. When adopting a 'hill climbing' strategy to school improvement, the failure to countenance the diversity and unpredictability of the school will limit success and, at worst, cause inadvertent harm.

To help school leaders take wiser action in the face of such complexity we suggest the following:

1. Recognise how your expertise affects your perspective on the problems you encounter. To what extent do the solutions you propose feed your self-efficacy?
2. Develop a more disciplined approach to school improvement efforts, which includes:
   A. a detailed exploration of the problem (including how the problem manifests, how it has evolved over time and how it is variously perceived);
   B. a more considered approach to implementing solutions (including a recognition of the regularities that the innovation may disrupt).
3. Try to experiment and iterate with tight feedback loops tied to reality. For example, after you 'introduce' a new system, can staff explain it? Can students explain it? How do they perceive and respond to it?
4. Continually question the effect your interventions are having upon the school (or schools) as experienced by students and teachers rather than merely an imagined, abstract, version of it.
5. Watch out for 'the waltz' between teachers and school leaders. Discuss this emergent behaviour with teachers and develop an organisational understanding about how it holds back genuine school improvement.
6. Treat dissenting voices as a valuable signal that there are different ways to make sense of the current situation. If staff are reluctant to change, why might this be? What might they risk losing if they adopt a proposed change?

Reflective questions

- What educational myths are persistent? To what extent are these really myths as opposed to ideas that are unfashionable, or simply contradict your world view?
- To what extent is there a perceptual gap between teachers and leaders about the problems faced by your school (or a school you know): both which problems should be prioritised and how these are defined?
- How often have you engaged in genuine dialogue about educational problems to develop a shared understanding of these problems?
- Can you think of examples of Maslow's Law of the Instrument whereby solutions are proposed that 'fit' with the expertise of the person proposing them?
- How often do school improvement efforts account for the regularities that an innovation will disrupt or replace in your experience?
- Do you recognise 'the waltz' that allows school leaders to remain in a state of complexity denial? What role have you played in this dance?

CHAPTER 10 – THE SENSE OF AN ENDING

What it seems to come to is this. Men in the middest make considerable imaginative investments in coherent patterns which, by the provision of an end, make possible a satisfying consonance with the origins and with the middle.

Frank Kermode, *The Sense of an Ending: Studies in the Theory of Fiction*[187]

The story we have told you about schooling is not the one we set out to write. The three of us came together through a shared feeling that the prevailing narrative about schools no longer made sense to us. We hoped to write a more truthful narrative about the way that schools are. The search for this truth served a purpose in motivating us to engage in the often effortful and frustrating act of writing. However, as we talked, wrote and edited together we began to realise that the absolute truth was less of a priority to us, or indeed an achievable pursuit.

The truth may be out there, but it is not all that is needed to motivate those working in education. All of us, whether as teachers, leaders or policymakers, have a need to make sense of our roles and daily experiences. We look for plausible stories to give meaning to our endeavours. Accuracy may be less important than a narrative that resonates with us: one that fits with the current climate, reduces equivocality, avoids disrupting work we are invested in and offers a better future.[188] Plausible narratives provide momentum, but they can also deceive and divert us.

In the quote at the start of this chapter, Frank Kermode writes about the theory of fiction, the narrative arcs we create to make sense of our own lives as just a short period in the history of the world. Where Kermode theorises about fiction, we have found ourselves thinking about the fiction of theory: the stories we tell ourselves about how the schooling system works and our role within it. Our little fictions masquerade as truths. Each policy wave washing over schools is the product of an appealing narrative about how the fundamental problems of schooling can be overcome. Every teacher holds in mind a story about their classes: the characters, their history, their destiny. They seek comfort that their career appears to offer a clear and unambiguous purpose: the chance to make a difference to the world. School leaders imagine their own story arc – often one in which they are the hero! – that plays out on the stage of their imagined school. Policymakers swoop in with solutions that the workers on the ground, they assume, are too naïve, obstinate or impotent to create for themselves. The stories we tell ourselves become our reality.

Alas, the stories we tell here have a whiff of tragedy about them, for the fundamental problems of schooling are never resolved. We have tried to avoid writing modern tragedies, ones in which an inherent flaw in the hero's character leads to their downfall. Modern tragedies are the kind of tragedies that Michael Gove, as Secretary of State, tried to write about teachers, the teaching unions and the educational 'Blob'.[189] Nicky Morgan, as a later Secretary of State, told a modern tragedy when she blamed teachers for writing off poor children through the 'soft bigotry of low expectations'.[190] Politicians tend to favour stories where teachers and leaders are the anti-heroes responsible for bringing the tragic end into being, for it readily points to a solution.

Instead, in this book we have tended towards the classical tragedy narrative with noble heroes struggling to make sense of their role, agency and influence as they strive to serve the needs of young people. Mistakes or faults are not intentional but instead derive from our heroes' circumstances or their simplistic and biased perceptions of reality.[191] Unlike classical tragedies, however, our stories have no end; we leave open the possibility that our heroes can rescue defeat from the jaws of failure if only they recognise in time the forces acting upon them.

Improving the imagined school

Throughout this book we have used the theoretical ideas of complexity and sense-making to characterise an inherently unknowable and uncertain education system inhabited by millions of interacting children, hundreds of thousands of diverse classrooms and teachers and thousands of unique institutions. This complexity, unknowledge and uncertainty means that practitioners, leaders and policymakers are continually wrongfooted in their attempts to overcome the fundamental problems of schooling.

The prevailing narrative about school improvement, influenced as it is by implementation science and assumptions about causal linearity, predictability and control, has been exposed as a reductive account of how the system changes. Ahistorical and mechanical stories of school improvement are situated in imagined schools that exist only in the minds of those charged with 'improving' them. In place of these accounts, we propose that schools are more complex than previously portrayed and so our control over the future is more fragile than we may feel comfortable admitting. Uncertainty is rife, but often ignored.

We talk so little about these issues of unknowledge, uncertainty and complexity in education that we lack the language and constructs to do so. We have given names to some phenomena in the hope that they may become a common language for discussing school improvement: the lock-step problem, metamorphic problems, unknowledge, procedural regularities, 'You Should Know This' moments and the imagined school, to name a few (others are listed in the glossary). If we notice these phenomena more readily and use these conceptual frames to make sense of unfolding events, the dissonance we experience may be less troublesome to us. For those doing the 'impossible job' of teaching, a little more peace of mind would be welcome.

However, we suspect that the dialogue about school improvement will not change, at least not very much or for very long. Complexity denial, including the dismissal of the recent history of Next Big Things, is an expedient response to the challenges of working within a complex system. Explanatory monopolisation often prevails as it affords a single lens with which to bring into focus discrete solutions to the problems we face. In doing so we can blur out signs of the nested complexity in which we work, denying or ignoring conflicting viewpoints. This allows us to maintain clear narratives about the problem and our capacity to resolve it. As T.S. Eliot wisely said: 'Humankind cannot bear very much reality.'[192]

However, simplistic expectations that deny complexity flounder when confronted with it. No leader, teacher or student can cope well, or for long, with the expectation that their daily lived experience should align neatly with such accounts. We all know of this dissonance between the imagined school and our daily experience, between the sacred accounts of our schools and the profane reality. As simple narratives crash against a complex reality, they cause the system to lurch from one 'solution' to another with individuals changing tack as increasingly desperate attempts to fix the system become untenable.

The Last Big Thing is dead. Long live the Next Big Thing! We make these decries with all the futility but none of the self-awareness of King Canute in holding back the tide. And we never seem to learn.

It lives!

As stories are important in education, so too are metaphors.[193] Complexity theory rejects machine metaphors that describe causal relationships as purposeful, linear and deterministic, instead leaning towards biological systems of interconnected and multi-layered processes that make prediction highly unreliable. It is therefore perhaps no surprise that, in writing this book, we have found ourselves returning again and again to imagining the education system as a living entity, a conscious beast, even, with its own character, intent and agency. The personification of the system casts it as a character in our story. Those working in and around the school system may be considered to have a relationship with it – one that evolves as each is adaptive to the other.

Of course, the education system is not a living thing, but this metaphor is appealing and may provide insights that are otherwise hidden. In chapter 1, we noted that so many aspects of schools have not changed across generations, as if the system pushes back against repeated attempts to reform it. In chapter 4, we saw what happened when chalkboards (and later interactive whiteboards) were imposed on an educational creature who did not ask for them. This biological approach can help us imagine how the after-school professional development sessions we saw in chapter 7 emerge as an adaptive response to the needs of the creature, helping an assistant head to feel agency in their school improvement role, while allowing teachers to let new ideas wash over them without disrupting who they are. Thus, where the mechanistic approach views such sessions as ineffective and dysfunctional because they fail to improve instructional practice, the biological approach suggests they are emergent and indeed functional within a system with complex needs.

We find a parallel metaphor in the depiction of Gaia, the personification of planet Earth. The Gaia hypothesis, proposed by the chemist James Lovelock, asserts that the living organisms on Earth interact with their inorganic surroundings to form a synergistic, self-regulating, complex system that creates and sustains the conditions needed for life.[194] The hypothesis is named after Gaia, the Greek goddess who personified Earth. While the theory is contested, it has enlightened our understanding of global symbiotic processes, such as that of global warming. One poetic offspring of the Gaia hypothesis is Daisyworld.

Daisyworld is a computer simulation developed by James Lovelock and Andrew Watson to illustrate the Gaia hypothesis.[195] In the simulation, there is a hypothetical world orbiting a star. On the world grow two varieties of daisy: white-petalled daisies that reflect light and black-petalled daisies that absorb light. The daisy population and the surface temperature of Daisyworld are observed through the simulation as the sun's rays become stronger and weaker. The surface temperature stays constant, despite the changing intensity of the sun's rays, as the populations of white- and black-petalled daisies grow and decline with a regulating effect. Daisyworld thus maintains the conditions for life through the adaptive responses of the living organisms. It is as if the world wants life to survive. It is one small step to imagine a beneficent deity, to personify the system, the metaphor a shorthand for a complex, dynamic process.

We might imagine our own simulated education system where teachers and pupils are the daisies, existing in a symbiotic relationship with the non-living system. Together the system achieves homeostasis, keeping the conditions of the creature as they need them to be despite external nudging or prodding. As accountability for exam outcomes grows, the desire for a broader definition of educational quality flourishes. As pressure to reduce exclusions increases, 'off-rolling' practices spike. As financial resources become more scarce, instructional techniques that are effective for larger class sizes come in vogue and a reliance on personalised approaches declines. As a pandemic forces isolation, the value placed on the social and emotional purpose of schooling increases. In each instance, the educational creature finds a way to survive. Mechanistic systems do not flex in such ways: they are 'controlled' but in a manner that can be rigid, unyielding and fragile. Our Gaia-like personification of a complex educational system is more fluid, responsive and self-sustaining, in response to our repeated attempts to disrupt it. This may leave us feeling powerless in the face of a creature that appears to have its own agency and volition, but it should not. We may be mere daisies, but we play a role in nurturing and maintaining the conditions for education to carry on.

By breathing metaphorical life into the school system, we might better understand why events unfold in the way that they do. We might learn to steer the system more successfully, working with the system rather than against it, becoming attuned to the creature's biological rhythms and systems. Importantly, we might come to terms with our impotence and unknowledge by recognising the limits of our control and insight.

There is a risk that we are too taken in by this naturalistic metaphor, as we are by the appeal of organic food and homeopathic medicine. Describing the school system organically gives it a wholesome feel that may be more comforting than instructive if we allow it to be. However, isn't it preferable to feel part of an entity with spirit and energy than to imagine ourselves to be a cog in an educational machine?

Describing the school system as an educational creature helps us imagine where Next Big Things come from. They emerge from the creature because they serve a purpose. Perhaps if we see fads as emergent rather than imposed, we can feel less threatened, we can embrace what feels useful to us and we can hold the new ideas loosely, knowing that a new Next Big Thing will emerge before long. And if Next Big Things are treated as emergent, we can try to guess what the Next Big Thing will be in future years. For each is a response to the situation the creature finds itself in, a response to the Last Big Thing, a rebalancing of the needs of the creature.

The fox and the hedgehog

We finish the book by considering how those of us working in and around the system – the teachers, school leaders and policymakers – should proceed. Let's start with those charged with making their school better for the young people who pass through it: the school leaders.

Fundamental to school leadership is the ability to make good decisions, which in turn depends on the ability to make sense of the present and predict how future events will play out. We have seen how fraught with difficulty this is. Leaders must make decisions despite realms of unknowledge, and frightening levels of complexity, uncertainty and diversity of belief and practice. We might hope that a leader in tune with the system might resist being swept along by the Next Big Thing, might countenance complexity, might treat their certainty with caution. But what sort of people can do this, and is this disposition one that can be fostered?

In his study of the predictive abilities of political scientists in anticipating the collapse of the USSR, Philip Tetlock found that the experts were no better at forecasting than the toss of a coin.[196] The reason, he surmised, is that making predictions about an inherently complex system requires the weaving together of various strands of thought and evidence, from multiple perspectives. Political thinkers and commentators simply took a position that was too fixed and partisan to appreciate the subtleties of the unfolding narrative. Tetlock verified his findings through surveys of a range of 'experts'. Interestingly, while predictive performance overall was poor across contexts, it was more so in those called upon by the media to give comment, and less so in those away from the spotlight. Through carrying out a series of personality tests, he was able to classify his experts along a spectrum. At one end of this spectrum was what he called hedgehogs and at the other, foxes.

In his book *The Signal and the Noise*, Nate Silver provides us with a description of the Hedgehog and Fox personality types.[197] Hedgehogs, he says, 'believe in Big Ideas'. Where they have lots of data available to them, they construct stories that are neat and easily told. These stories have polarised characters (good guys and bad guys), simple themes and a satisfying resolution. Hedgehogs are typically specialised, stalwart, stubborn, order-seeking, confident and ideological. They come across well on TV as they portray certainty and assurance. While this certainty is appealing, it is easy for the narrative to crowd out critical thinking and for the nuance to be lost.

Foxes, on the other hand, are 'scrappy little creatures who believe in a plethora of little ideas and in taking a multitude of approaches toward a problem'. They are multi-disciplinary, adaptable, self-critical, cautious, empirical, open to challenge and tolerant of complexity. When foxes have lots of data available to them, they are cautious about the false signals hidden within the noise. Crucially, Silver argues, they 'know more about what they don't know'. Such characters are *less* likely to draw us in with their charisma and with a compelling story that enlightens us. However, their estimates about the future, while less unequivocal, are more likely to come true. Their decisions and actions are therefore hedged bets, and they are poised to change course should the future unfold in unpredictable ways.

If we accept, as we argued above, that schools need plausible (not just accurate) stories to provide momentum, then we might question whether the 'scrappy little creature' portrayed will capture the heart as well as the mind of the workforce. While charisma alone is insufficient, the ability to tell a good story – one that captures the imagination and propels us to action – is surely desirable, even if that story deceives us into thinking things are more knowable and certain than they truly are.

School leaders, we suggest, must channel their inner fox and outer hedgehog. They must 'keep it sophisticatedly simple',[198] both countenancing complexity and offering a compelling narrative about the future. Or more pithily, we might say, 'don't oversimplify the problems; don't overcomplicate the response'.[199]

The complex and the simple

Ultimately, teachers and schools must *do something* to make progress, which means harnessing the energy of pupils and staff towards achieving a goal. In this regard, a clear and simple plan and narrative is expedient. Seeking out simple solutions to complicated (rather than complex) problems that can be isolated, clearly defined and for which there are known effective interventions may help us improve some aspects of education. Every day there is an example of a school that has made a small, simple change to improve pupils' experience. These can work very well, for example, where they seek to target an increase in achieved student learning time, an output that has currency regardless of the age of child or subject being taught. However, while simplicity of thought and deed may help us improve certain aspects of education that can be isolated and clearly defined, it is likely to fail us when applied to complex, intractable problems. In many aspects of school improvement work we cannot avoid confronting the emergent behaviours of the system, and it is in these large, messy areas where good advice runs short.

We cannot expect schools to give up on the kind of large-scale school improvement strategies that can easily get lost in translation from Big Idea to practical implementation. Idealised aims, along with a mechanical explanation for how to realise them, come into conflict with the messy reality of schools. We might adopt an ambitious plan for mixed-ability grouping in maths premised on an imagined world where all children will feel more motivated to progress through the curriculum in lock-step fashion, only to find that their differing starting points and the demand placed on teachers' time and expertise mean that even more students fall behind. We might design rigorous tracking systems to identify where children are struggling and select 'proven' intervention strategies to rectify this, only to discover that our codified data is a poor proxy for learning and our interventions lack the promised impact. Or we might bring in sweeping curriculum reforms to give pupils access to 'the best that has been thought and said',[200] only to later realise that many lack either the schema or the motivation to consume such powerful knowledge. Grand ambition is often undermined by over-simplification and an underestimation of how hard it is for reform to gain traction. A simple, modest plan may be preferable to a simplistic, ambitious one.

Anticipating the troubles of school improvement and deliberately looking for the inevitable frictional encounter with reality might help avoid the crass implementation efforts and complexity denying waltz that we considered in chapters 8 and 9, respectively. We should learn to expect, rather than fear, information, suggesting that the process is not working quite as we planned it to. The leader's task becomes one of judging whether a fresh compromise with the fundamental problems of schooling is preferable to that which it replaces. This encourages nuanced, iterative decision making rather more than the impossible task of designing a one-shot solution to fully resolve the fundamental problems once and for all.

Despite the background noise of complexity, there are still problems to solve in schools that are concrete, discrete and can be worked on in isolation. It can be cathartic to spend time on these and to see tangible progress being made. School leaders may choose to increase their presence to ensure a more orderly transition of pupils between lessons. Teachers can strengthen the start of lessons by adopting and regularising simple routines. Teaching assistants can be asked to listen to a child read aloud each week to build their confidence and comprehension. Librarians can adopt a labelling system to help students and teachers select appropriate texts to read. Pastoral staff may train in de-escalation techniques to calm agitated students and diffuse conflict. It is not always necessary to grapple with big educational questions or to make grand plans to achieve gains in educational standards. Modest, incremental, uncontentious actions, when aggregated over time, may achieve more than the most ambitious school improvement strategy. We might imagine a future school as one that is slightly better than before in a range of respects. This is a vision that all parties can buy into. School improvement may be a balance between the Next Small Thing and a messy, opaque, evolutionary adaptation of the educational creature.

But if our role is to 'design' the future, to dream up the Next Big Thing or imagine the policy solution that will 'fix' the system, what then? Pity the policymaker charged with taming the educational beast.

The emergence of policy

In England, most Secretaries of State for Education arrive to the job knowing little about education beyond their own (often private) schooling. The little knowledge they do have can be a dangerous thing, producing pet policies in the image of some experience they had themselves and generally causing them to overestimate the ability of education to transform society. Overestimating their ability to deliver on this brief, and empowered by their own educational success, they launch themselves naïvely into battle with the beast, holding a raft of policies as weapons. Faced with the successive failure of past education policies to transform standards, the temptation is to pull hard on policy levers to bring about ambitious and disruptive reform.

If this is the choice they make, then so be it. But the path of reform will almost certainly not be in the direction anticipated. For they know little of the educational beast they are about to encounter, of how successive governments in England have created a creature more complex than in almost any other country in the world, with dozens of unique institutional arrangements, thousands of non-governmental providers, legally binding autonomy and limited levers for central government to pull on to affect change. The decentralisation in the English education system is not necessarily damaging, for it acts as a good hedge against poor centralised decision making. But it does mean the nature and pace of policy change is necessarily curtailed.

Secretaries of State turn to experts and advisers to help them transform schools and those who knock most loudly on their door will be the hedgehogs, the experts who are most convinced that they have answers for how to transform the system. Their certainty might arise from naivety – perhaps they are simply political analysts fresh from their philosophy, politics and economics (PPE) degrees using the education system as a testing ground for their idealism or they are junior academics who have dug themselves so deeply into research in a single policy area that it is hard to countenance other solutions. Their certainty might arise from commercial interests – perhaps they are educational charities or businesses with a 'big idea' that will conveniently transform schools alongside their own balance sheet. Perhaps their certainty is their stock trade, as it is for management consultancy companies such as McKinsey, where a former employee was once told: 'We're billing clients 500 grand a year, so you have to be sure of what you are saying.'[201]

The scholar John Gall gave the following advice, which is pertinent to education policymakers:[202]

> *A complex system that works is invariably found to have evolved from a simple system that worked. A complex system designed from scratch never works and cannot be patched up to make it work. You have to start over, beginning with a working simple system.*

It is undoubtedly tempting to propose grand reforms, predicated on appealing narratives about what schools are or have become. However, policy that sets out to tame the beast inevitably fails to do so. The most complex, all-embracing instruments of control have the weakest effects on a system that has evolved to wax and wane in response to demands placed on it. Far better, as Gall suggests, to seed evolution through small-scale, localised system reform. This is not to say that policymakers should ignore the complex problems that frustrate them, rather that they seek to address these problems by leveraging that which can be leveraged, which may mean taking a narrow approach to designing a policy or process of change. Policymakers must then countenance complexity as they estimate and imagine how the system will adapt to their attempt to steer it.

However, even while implementing small-scale system reform, 'coherence' research suggests that the interaction and alignment of the system should be constantly monitored. Even for a simple policy, it will be the complex and constant interaction of factors in the system that determines its outcomes. To illustrate this, consider the introduction of funding for tuition in response to the pandemic, much of which will be delivered outside normal school hours. While there is good evidence to suggest that one-to-one or small group tuition can increase attainment for pupils, its success at a local level will depend on many factors.[203] In some contexts, safe transport home may not be available, or it may be difficult to employ suitable staff. There may be established extracurricular activities that pupils are required to forgo to participate in study. Older pupils may have responsibilities to care for younger siblings, attend part-time work or experience peer pressure to hang out after school. After-school study may 'work' in theory, or in certain situations, but without careful attention to local context it may become an expensive and time-consuming failed initiative.

A visit to the museum

How can we help advisers to a Secretary of State give better advice? In the introduction to this book, we showcased our museum of educational failure. This museum should be the first place a new Secretary of State or policy adviser visits on taking up their post. What might a visit to the museum reveal?

First, we might learn that policymaking is about more than a good idea; policies must stand the test of time. We should encourage policymakers to spend less time looking for ideas that are transformative and more time worrying about whether their innovations will stick around! Time matters because even policies that attempt to change the system in discrete and specific ways may take more than a decade to achieve their intended effect. A good example is the now universal use of systematic synthetic phonics to teach young children to read in England. Against a background of decades of research and experimentation by academics and companies working in the field,[204] it was formally proposed by the Rose Review in 2006,[205] slowly piloted and rolled out across local authorities until 2009–10,[206] bankrolled to near universal provision by a new government from 2011,[207] turbocharged by accountability through the phonics test from summer 2012[208] and yet the policy framework to maintain its provision is still being tweaked in 2021.[209] Policy success can only be measured in decades, not years.

Policies that successfully persist may not be the most perfect ones on paper. The combustion engine is a mucky, inefficient way of propelling a vehicle, and thankfully we are on the verge of consigning it to history. However, it has lasted, and its longevity has allowed an infinite number of adaptations to flourish – industrial specialisation, mobility of labour, social integration and globalisation, to name but a few not insignificant evolutionary and revolutionary changes. Policies that persist should not be underestimated, even if they are not the perfect solution to a complex problem. A policy need not even work that well, as long as it keeps us moving forward for, without knowing it, we might have created the conditions for something else to emerge later. That is not to say we should be unconcerned about designing policy that has impact, just less fretful if it does not immediately appear to achieve what we thought it would. Time is a necessary condition for emergent solutions to evolve.

The path that a new policy goes on will necessarily be a bumpy one, so the policies that last must be anti-fragile. Whereas fragile things break under stress, anti-fragile things can withstand or even benefit from it, growing and adapting as they encounter hurdles. As Nassim Nicholas Taleb points out, this means being resistant to disorder, and disorder is a function of time and exposure.[210] Therefore, the real test of the quality of a thing (an idea, theory, policy) is how well it resists the ravages of time. Fragile things may survive while they can avoid contact with reality, but then collapse quite suddenly (like when the cup is dropped on a hard surface). Anti-fragile things will have the quality of growing and adapting as they are exposed to reality. If the acid test of a policy's quality is its longevity, we should look to those that have endured and evolved to learn the art of policy design. In this category we might put terminal examinations, INSET days, the national curriculum, Ofsted, school choice, the pattern of the school year and a curriculum structured around subjects. Each of these has been the subject of reform, critique and even attack, but have survived by adapting to these stressors. We may not like these features of the system, but we cannot deny their longevity.

The second thing a visit to the museum of educational failure may teach us is that, to make policy successful in practice, there must be a better understanding by policymakers about what makes schools tick. Policy enactment requires a mechanism, therefore good policy will have a coherent mid-level theory that guides implementation. Only teachers and school leaders can provide this insight to policymakers, and policy formulation without the involvement of frontline professionals will likely be ill-informed. Teachers can help identify the problems that are amenable to intervention, and that will make a meaningful difference to educational outcomes. Teachers can anticipate the contextual factors that will trip up generic policy. Teachers know where the grit is in the system that will frustrate implementation. On display in our museum of failure should be the story of Antaeus, son of Gaia, who derived his power by keeping contact with his mother, Earth. In the same way, we should teach advisers that policy has no power without it being in touch with the complex reality of the school system. Their role is not to act on the system, but to interact with it.[211]

Teachers are the experts as they have both the domain-specific expertise and localised knowledge. The denial of a teacher-voice in policymaking in England is symbolic of a denial of complexity and lack of respect for expertise. Combined with the need to take a long view on policymaking, with policy alignment stretching over more than one parliamentary session, at least some aspects of educational policy making may best be made by a semi-autonomous or a cross-party unit, supported by teachers on extended secondments, and not directly under the control of the Secretary of State. As things stand, there is no political incentive to play the long game and we cannot rely on ministers to prioritise their moral responsibility to lay the foundations for long-term educational reform over the need to convince voters that they are being 'tough on standards' or 'reducing attainment gaps'.

Nothing we propose can 'solve' the challenges of educational policymaking, for the fundamental problems of schooling cannot be solved, there are domains of unknowledge that may forever be beyond our grasp and the diversity and complexity of the school system makes concepts like control irrelevant. These are not palatable ideas for politicians, but they are nonetheless true. We would, therefore, be more successful at improving educational outcomes for children if we stretched the timescales of our policy thinking, designed targeted policy instruments to solve specific problems and were prepared to adapt to the unforeseen effects of policy implementation.

The sense of an ending

While it may not be possible to tame the educational beast, we may at least learn to live with it. The key to doing so is to come to terms with our unknowledge and uncertainty as we make sense of the complex reality of the school system. Our conclusions are not definitive, but we believe they are plausible.

You may not be any more certain having read this book, but we hope you are a little wiser. We have perhaps raised questions rather than provided answers. However, there is strength in resisting the definitive. In the words of Professor Yuval Noah Harari, 'Questions you cannot answer are usually far better for you than answers you cannot question.'[212]

Schools can exist in a state of complexity denial, but it is perhaps better that they do not. We wish for school improvement to be straightforward – for the Next Big Thing to solve the fundamental problems of schooling – but it isn't and it won't. It is foolish to deny this complexity, but faint-hearted to be defeated by it. We may still find simple, modest ways to improve the school system without resorting to the simplistic, grand gestures that characterise many past efforts. This sentiment is captured eloquently in the following quote by Supreme Court Justice Oliver Wendell Holmes,[213] and affords a sense of an ending to our narrative about schools:

> *For the simplicity on this side of complexity, I wouldn't give you a fig. But for the simplicity on the other side of complexity, for that I would give you anything I have.*

GLOSSARY

Adaptive agents	Individuals whose behaviours adapt to the behaviour of others and the wider system. The response of adaptive agents evolves as they receive information from the environment about the success or failure of their adaptations. See also **Feedback loops**.
Bounded rationality	A decision that is rational given the limited knowledge held by the decision maker.
Cargo cult	The belief that copying the mechanisms associated with receiving benefits will itself bring about these benefits. The term derives from the belief that developed in a Melanesian tribe that building runways would bring about the arrival of a miraculous 'cargo' of goods from supernatural sources, based on the observation of supplies being delivered by aircraft to colonial officials.
(The) class as an abstraction	Attributing attributes or behaviours to a class of children that homogenises the group and ignores the diversity of those within it.

Coalition of advocates	Interest groups with varying motivations and goals who coalesce around a policy idea. These ideas may offer an appealing solution to a perceived problem. To appeal to such a wide range of parties, the solution will be necessarily poorly defined. See also **Explanatory monopolisation**.
Complex system	A system that behaves in ways that cannot be explained with reference only to the properties of its component parts.
Complexity denial	Assuming the system is more known, more predictable and more controllable than it truly is. This denial may be due to an inability to comprehend this complexity, or it may be an adaptive response as it is expedient to avoid countenancing this complexity.
Complexity theory	A branch of systems theory that examines the emergent behaviours of biological, physical and social systems. See also **Emergence**.
Compliancy expertise	The development of knowledge and skill in responding to external demands in such a way that signals compliance but avoids disruption to established beliefs and behaviours.
Creeping managerialism	Increasing levels of control by managers in response to perceived deficiencies in how subordinates carry out organisational functions.
Emergence	The behaviours and properties of a system that are not explainable with reference to the behaviour of the component parts of the system.

Ex ante case-specific causal models	Realist models for predicting what will happen as the result of an intervention. 'Ex ante' because they are for before-the-fact prediction; 'case-specific' because they are solely concerned with local prediction rather than general rules; 'causal' because they aim to trace out a web of possible causal processes.
Explanatory monopolisation	This occurs when a coalition of advocates simultaneously subscribe to the plausibility of an idea. See also **Coalition of advocates**.
Feedback loops	Information from the environment that is fed back into a system with the effect of either amplifying (positive) or counteracting (negative) effects.
(The) fundamental problems of schooling	The irresolvable dilemmas that are an inevitable consequence of the way the system is set up and the expectations placed upon it. See also the **Invisibility of learning** and the **Lock-step problem**.
Helicopter drops	A randomised approach to searching for promising ideas.
Hill climbing	Gains made by incrementally improving specific aspects of the system without knowing the extent of improvement that can be achieved.
Ill-fated solution	A solution that is destined to fail as it attempts to solve irresolvable problems. See also **Irresolvable dilemma**.
(The) illusion of explanatory depth	A false assumption that familiarity with a concept or process equates to a detailed understanding of the mechanism that produces it.

(The) imagined school	A mental model that, due to the limits of the human mind and the reductive process of sensemaking, is a simplified version of the actual school. This imagined school may become the object of school leaders' interventions. See also the **Illusion of explanatory depth**.
Invisibility of learning	Learning is a phenomenon that cannot ever be fully known or measured.
Irresolvable dilemma	A problem that does not have a solution.
Law of the Instrument	A cognitive bias towards defining problems as amenable to solution by familiar tools and personal expertise. Often attributed to Abraham Maslow; 'If the only tool you have is a hammer, it is tempting to treat everything as if it were a nail.'[214]
(The) lesson as an abstraction	A single lesson as envisaged by a teacher can only function as an abstracted simplification of the disparate experiences (and learning) experienced by individual members of the class.
Lock-step problem	The need to educate large numbers of children in a defined body of knowledge, and finite timescale, while acknowledging their different starting points and pace at which they can acquire this knowledge. This problem is a consequence of a mass education system and is typically resolved through grouping children in classes and teaching them in lock-step fashion.
Mandatory miracle	An imposed solution that is intended to solve one of the fundamental problems of schooling but does not contain the instructions for how to do so.

Metamorphic problems	The phenomenon whereby an attempt to solve a persistent problem has the effect that the problem re-emerges in a form that bears the hallmarks of the previous solution. See also **Persistent problems.**
Naïve intervention	A term coined by the economist Nassim Taleb to describe the harmful unintended consequences of well-meaning actions taken in ignorance of complexity.
Nested systems	Embedded sub-systems that interconnect such that events have repercussions at various levels throughout the system.
Patch-making behaviour	Expending disproportionate amounts of time trying to fix errors rather than address the root causes of these errors.
Patches	Corrective actions that address the symptom and not the cause. See also **Patch-making behaviour.**
Persistent problems	A term coined in an educational context by Mary Kennedy to mean the universal and eternal problems that beset teachers in carrying out their role. The term is used more broadly in this book to mean the universal and eternal problems that beset schools. See also **Irresolvable dilemma.**
Personalised learning	Any attempt to meet the individual needs of a child through the education system.
Plausible stories	A narrative about events that resonates and facilitates action.

Pluralistic ignorance	A misperception about what others in a group commonly believe or do. When many members of a group hold the same misperception, a gap between the actual and perceived group norm exists. Teachers may believe that the latest policy makes sense to others and that they are outliers. If this belief is generally held, there will be a conspiracy of silence in the face of non-sensical demands.
Policy waves	Successive educational policies that impact on schools before receding and being replaced by the next big idea or initiative.
Private narratives	The stories we tell ourselves to make sense of events that happen to us.
Procedural regularities	The habits and routines that define a school's daily operations. Regularities are handrails for behaviour that enable people within the organisation to function without continual decision making.
Professional isolation	Limited opportunities for professional dialogue and collaboration, which means teachers are rarely exposed to new ideas or critical perspectives on their own practices.
Public narratives	The stories we co-construct to make sense of events.
Reification	The process by which abstract concepts or procedural regularities come to be considered concrete and necessary. Colloquially speaking it occurs when something becomes 'a thing'. See also **Procedural regularities**.

School complexity	The product of their interconnections with other institutions; the presence of adaptive agents; the effect of feedback loops; and the existence of nested systems. See also **Adaptive agents**, **Feedback loops** and **Nested systems**.
Sensemaking	A psychological process whereby individuals interpret experience in relation to their prior frames of reference.
Shadow boxing	Attempting to solve illusory problems and acting on an imagined version of the world that is only loosely connected to reality.
Unknowledge	Defined areas of ignorance.
(The) waltz	The metaphorical dance between those in authority and their subordinates in which both parties are complicit in maintaining an illusion that anything meaningful is occurring and that school improvement is actually quite simple.
You Should Do This	The instructions school leaders give to teachers about how they should perform their roles. These instructions are in part a consequence of an interventionist identity that forms around school leaders.
You Should Know This	An exclamation by teachers that is symptomatic of the exasperation they feel in confronting the lock-step problem.

ENDNOTES

1. Karr, J.-B.A. (1862). *Les Guêpes* [in French]. Paris, France: Michel Lévy Frères (p. 278).
2. Learn more about Toaster Eggs in: Lidz, F. (2017, December). There's a giant warehouse full of product launches that failed. *Smithsonian Magazine*. Retrieved from https://www.smithsonianmag.com/innovation/where-to-go-to-buy-failed-products-180967221/
   The other products are mentioned in:
   Burkeman, O. (2012, 15 June). Happiness is a glass half empty. *The Guardian*. Retrieved from https://www.theguardian.com/lifeandstyle/2012/jun/15/happiness-is-being-a-loser-burkeman
3. If you would like to know more about The Museum of Failed Products, the story is told here:
   Burkeman, O. (2012, 15 June). Happiness is a glass half empty. *The Guardian*. Retrieved from https://www.theguardian.com/lifeandstyle/2012/jun/15/happiness-is-being-a-loser-burkeman
4. West, M., Ainscow, M., Wigelsworth, M. & Troncoso, P. (2017). *Challenge the Gap: Evaluation Report*. Education Endowment Foundation Report. Retrieved from https://educationendowmentfoundation.org.uk/projects-and-evaluation/projects/challenge-the-gap/;
   Institute for Effective Education (2016). *Teacher Effectiveness Enhancement Programme: Evaluation Report*. Education Endowment Foundation Report. Retrieved from https://educationendowmentfoundation.org.uk/projects-and-evaluation/

projects/teacher-effectiveness-enhancement-programme/;
Humphrey, N., Squires, G., Choudry, S., Byrne, E., Demkowicz, O., Troncoso, P. & Wo, L. (2020). *Achievement for All: Evaluation Report.* Education Endowment Foundation Report. Retrieved from https://educationendowmentfoundation.org.uk/projects-and-evaluation/projects/achievement-for-all/

5. Schueler, B.E., Armstrong Asher, C., Larned, K.E., Mehrotra, S. & Pollard, C. (2020). Improving low-performing schools: a meta-analysis of impact evaluation studies. *EdWorkingPaper (Annenberg Institute, Brown University)*, 20(274). DOI: 10.26300/qxjk-yq91; Golann, J.W. (2021). *Scripting the Moves: Culture and Control in a 'No-Excuses' Charter School.* Princeton, NJ: Princeton University Press.

6. Nye, P. (2020, 6 February). Secondary MAT league tables 2019: we need to talk about context [Blog post]. https://ffteducationdatalab.org.uk/2020/02/secondary-mat-league-tables-2019-we-need-to-talk-about-context/;
    Nye, P. (2019, 13 December). Primary MAT league tables 2019: comparing reading, writing and maths progress scores [Blog post]. https://ffteducationdatalab.org.uk/2019/12/primary-mat-league-tables-2019-comparing-reading-writing-and-maths-progress-scores
    For an example of a high-performing MAT chain that has failed to turnaround a school see:
    Belger, T. (2021, 11 June). England's largest academy trust gives up struggling school [News post]. *Schools Week.* Retrieved from https://schoolsweek.co.uk/englands-largest-academy-trust-gives-up-struggling-school/

7. Figure 2 shows information on post-inspection exam results:
    Allen, R. & Burgess, S. (2012). *How Should We Treat Under-performing Schools? A Regression Discontinuity Analysis of School Inspections in England.* CMPO Working Paper No. 12/87. Retrieved from https://www.bristol.ac.uk/media-library/sites/cmpo/migrated/documents/wp287.pdf

8. Sarason, S.B. (1971). *The Culture of the School and the Problem of Change.* Boston, MA: Allyn and Bacon.

9. Klein, G., Moon, B. & Hoffman, R.R. (2006). Making sense of sensemaking 1: alternative perspectives. *IEE Intelligent Systems,* 21(4) (July/August), 70–71.
10. King James Bible (2011). *Holy Bible: King James Version (KJV).* (Original work published 1611.)
11. *The Washington Post* (1984, 29 January). The 6 o'clock scholar: librarian of Congress Daniel Boorstin and his love affair with books by Carol Krucoff, start page K1, quote page K8, column 2, Washington, D.C.
12. There are many models of complex human systems that have relevance to the education system. See, for example: Gell-Mann, M. (1994). Complex adaptive systems. In Cowan, G. & Pines, D. (Eds.) *Complexity: Metaphors, Models and Reality* (pp. 17–45). New York, NY: Perseus Books.
    Mitleton-Kelly, E. & Davy, L.K. (2013). The concept of 'co-evolution' and its application in the social sciences: a review of the literature. In Mitleton-Kelly, E. (Ed.) *Co-evolution of Intelligent Socio-technical Systems: Modelling and Applications in Large Scale Emergency and Transport Domains.* Berlin, Germany: Springer;
    Weick, K.E. (1976). Educational organizations as loosely coupled systems. *Administrative Science Quarterly,* 21(1), 1–19.
13. We closely follow the description of complexity in educational institutions described by: Ghaffarzadegan, N., Larson, R. & Hawley, J. (2017). Education as a complex system. *Systems Research and Behavioral Science,* 34(3), 211–215. DOI: 10.1002/sres.2405
14. Holland, J.H. (2014). *Complexity: A Very Short Introduction.* Oxford, UK: Oxford University Press.
15. Stacey, R. (1996). *Complexity and Creativity in Organisations.* San Francisco, CA: Berrett-Koeller.
16. Cook, R.I. (2000). How complex systems fail [Blog post]. https://how.complexsystems.fail/
17. Eoyand, G.H. & Holladay, R.J. (2013). *Adaptive Action: Leveraging Uncertainty in Your Organization.* Redwood City, CA: Stanford University Press (p. 18).
18. Coe, R. & Tymms, P. (2008). Summary of research on changes in educational standards in the UK. In Harris, M. (Ed.) *Education*

Briefing Book 2008: IoD Policy Paper. London, UK: Institute of Directors;

Coe, R. (2013, 18 June). *Improving Education: A Triumph of Hope over Experience* [Speech transcript], Durham University, UK;

Coe, R. (2009). School improvement: reality and illusion. *British Journal of Educational Studies*, 57(4), 363–379. DOI: 10.1111/j.1467-8527.2009.00444.x;

Shayer, M., Ginsburg, D. & Coe, R. (2007). Thirty years on – a large anti-Flynn effect? The Piagetian test volume & heaviness norms 1975–2003. *British Journal of Educational Psychology*, 77(1), 25–41;

Tymms, P. & Merrell, C. (2007). *Standards and Quality in English Primary Schools Over Time: The National Evidence* (Primary Review Research Survey 4/1), Cambridge, UK: University of Cambridge Faculty of Education;

Hodgen, J., Kuchemann, D., Brown, M. & Coe, R. (2009). Children's understandings of algebra 30 years on. *Research in Mathematics Education*, 11(2), 193–194;

Hodgen, J., Küchemann, D., Brown, M. & Coe, R. (2010). Multiplicative reasoning, ratio and decimals: a 30-year comparison of lower secondary students' understandings. In Pinto, M.F. & Kawaski, T.F. (Eds.) *Proceedings of the 34th Conference of the International Group of the Psychology of Mathematics Education,* Durham, NJ: International Group for the Psychology of Mathematics Education, 3 (pp. 89–96).

19. The word 'unknowledge' is an old term with roots at least as far back as the 14th century. More recently, it has been used across several social science disciplines in the manner we describe. See, for example:
Schnick, I.C. (1999). *The Erotic Margin.* New York, NY: Verso;
Ford, J.L. (1990). Shackle's theory of decision-making under uncertainty: a brief exposition and critical assessment. In Frowen, S.F. (Eds.) *Unknowledge and Choice in Economics.* London, UK: Palgrave Macmillan.

20. Peck, M.S. (1978). *The Road Less Traveled: A New Psychology of Love, Traditional Values and Spiritual Growth.* New York, NY: Simon & Schuster.

21. Berube, Maurice R. (1994). *American School Reform: Progressive, Equity, and Excellence Movements, 1883–1993.* Westport, CT: Praeger (p. 21).

22. Rice, J.M. (1913). *Scientific Management in Education.* New York, NY: Publishers Printing Company (p. 1).

23. Walker, H. (1956). Methods of research. *Review of Educational Research,* 26(3), 323–343. DOI: 10.2307/1169365

24. Rice, J.M. (1898). *The Rational Spelling Book.* New York, NY: American Book Company.
    For discussion of his work, see:
    Stanley, J. (1966). Rice as a pioneer educational researcher. *Journal of Educational Measurement,* 3(2), 135–139. Retrieved from http://www.jstor.org/stable/1433888

25. Hattie, J. (2008). *Visible Learning: A Synthesis of over 800 Meta-analyses Relating to Achievement.* Abingdon, UK: Routledge.

26. Summarised in this opinion article by:
    Fletcher-Wood, H. (2021, 26 April). Research: is all our evidence all it's cracked up to be? *Schools Week.* Retrieved from https://schoolsweek.co.uk/research-is-all-our-evidence-its-cracked-up-to-be/.

27. See here for a critique of similar tools in the US:
    Dues, J.A. (2020, 6 January). Why evidence-based practices don't work: part I [Blog post]. https://fordhaminstitute.org/national/commentary/why-evidence-based-practices-dont-work-part-i

28. Kraft, M.A. (2020). Interpreting effect sizes of education interventions. *Educational Researcher,* 49(4), 241–253;
    Cheung, A.C. & Slavin, R.E. (2016). How methodological features affect effect sizes in education. *Educational Researcher,* 45(5), 283–292.

29. Elliott, V., Baird, J., Hopfenbeck, T.N., Ingram, J., Thompson, I., Usher, N., Zantout, M., Richardson, J. & Coleman, R. (2016). *A Marked Improvement? A Review of the Evidence on Written Marking.* Education Endowment Foundation Report. Retrieved from https://educationendowmentfoundation.org.uk/evidence-summaries/evidence-reviews/written-marking/

30. Goldacre, B. (2013). *Building Evidence into Education.* Retrieved from https://www.gov.uk/government/news/building-evidence-into-education.
31. This list is drawn from the headline results of EEF RCTs that can be found here:
Education Endowment Foundation (2021). Completed Projects [website]. Retrieved from https://educationendowmentfoundation.org.uk/projects-and-evaluation/reports/
32. Lortie-Forgues, H. and Inglis, M. (2019). Rigorous large-scale educational RCTs are often uninformative: should we be concerned? *Educational Researcher*, 48(3), 158–166. DOI:10.3102/0013189X19832850
33. Ioannidis, J.P.A. (2005). Why most published research findings are false. *PLoS Medicine,* 2(8), e124. DOI: 10.1371/journal.pmed.0020124
34. We calculated these figures by using counting trials tagged by EEF as for key stage 1 or 2 and those tagged as 'Effectiveness Trials' within the following website:
Education Endowment Foundation (2021). Completed Projects [website]. Retrieved from https://educationendowmentfoundation.org.uk/projects-and-evaluation/reports/
35. Boulay, B., Goodson, B., Olsen, R., McCormick, R., Darrow, C., Frye, M., Gan, K., Harvill, E. & Sarna, M. (2018). *The Investing in Innovation Fund: Summary of 67 Evaluations (Final Report).* US Department of Education Report. Retrieved from https://ies.ed.gov/ncee/pubs/20184013/pdf/20184013.pdf
36. Berliner, D.C. (2002). Educational research: the hardest science of all. *Educational Researcher*, 31(18), 18–20. DOI: 10.3102/0013189X031008018.
37. We took this language from analysis of health systems by: Braithwaite, J., Churruca, K., Long, J.C., Ellis, L.A. & Herkes, J. (2018). When complexity science meets implementation science: a theoretical and empirical analysis of systems change. *BMC Medicine*, 16(63). DOI: 10.1186/s12916-018-1057-z.

38. Boxer, A. (2019, 8 August). It's just a tool! Does everything work somewhere? [Blog post]. https://achemicalorthodoxy.wordpress. com/2019/08/08/its-just-a-tool-does-everything-work-somewhere/

39. Mawhin, J. (1998). Review of Poincaré and the three-body problem. *Isis*, 89(2), 345–346.

40. The two Grammar for Writing RCTs can be found here:
Torgerson, D., Torgerson, C., Mitchell, N., Buckley, H., Ainsworth, H., Heaps, C. & Jefferson, L. (2014). *Grammar for Writing: Evaluation Report and Executive Summary*. Education Endowment Foundation. Retrieved from https:// educationendowmentfoundation.org.uk/projects-and-evaluation/ projects/grammar-for-writing/;
Tracey, L., Boehnke, J.R. Elliott, L., Thorley, K., Ellison, S. & Bowyer-Crane, C. (2019). *Grammar for Writing: Evaluation Report and Executive Summary*. Education Endowment Foundation. Retrieved from https://educationendowmentfoundation.org.uk/projects-and-evaluation/projects/grammar-for-writing-effectiveness-trial/

41. Humphrey, N., Squires, G., Choudry, S., Byrne, E., Demkowicz, O., Troncoso, P. & Wo, L. (2020). *Achievement for All: Evaluation Report*. Education Endowment Foundation. Retrieved from https:// educationendowmentfoundation.org.uk/projects-and-evaluation/ projects/achievement-for-all/

42. Open Science Collaboration (2015). Estimating the reproducibility of psychological science. *Science*, 349(6251), aac4716. DOI: 10.1126/ science.aac4716

43. Makel, M.C. & Plucker, J.A. (2014). Facts are more important than novelty: replication in the education sciences. *Educational Researcher*, 43(6), 304–316. DOI:10.3102/0013189X14545513

44. Smaldino, P. (2019). Better methods can't make up for mediocre theory. *Nature*, 575(7781), 9. DOI: 10.1038/d41586-019-03350-5

45. This pre-registration has limited the extent to which researchers can data mine through choice of statistical models, exclusion of outliers, sub-group analysis, outcome switching and HARKing (hypothesising after the results are known).

46. Lanham, H.J., Leykum, L.K., Taylor, B.S., McCannon, C.J., Lindberg, C. & Lester, R.T. (2013). How complexity science can inform

scale-up and spread in health care: understanding the role of self-organization in variation across local contexts. *Social Science and Medicine*, 93, 194–202.

47. The only way to avoid spending more money on each trial would be to encourage schools to agree to within-school randomisation to a greater extent. Given most trials don't work better than existing practice, the moral arguments against favouring a random set of pupils in a school over another set is quite weak.

48. Greenhalgh, T. & Papoutsi, C. (2019). Spreading and scaling up innovation and improvement, *BMJ*, 365, l2068. DOI: 10.1136/bmj.l2068

49. See, for example, Lupton, R. & Hayes, D. (2021). *Great Mistakes in Education Policy: And How to Avoid Them in the Future*. Bristol, UK: Policy Press.

50. Cartwright, N. & Hardie, J. (2017). Predicting what will happen when you intervene. *Clinical Social Work Journal*, 45(3), 270–279 (p. 270). DOI: 10.1007/s10615-016-0615-0

51. Blastland, M. (2019) *The Hidden Half: How the World Conceals its Secrets*. London, UK: Atlantic Books.

52. Yang, C., Luo, L., Vadillo, M., Yu, R. & Shanks, D.R. (2020). Testing (quizzing) boosts classroom learning: A systematic and meta-analytic review. *Psychological Bulletin*, 147(4), 399–435. DOI: http://dx.doi.org/10.1037/bul0000309

53. For a critical perspective on the possibility of establishing general laws of learning and memory, see:
Roediger, H.L. (2008). Relativity of remembering: why the laws of memory vanished. *Annual Review of Psychology*, 59, 225–254. DOI: 10.1146/annurev.psych.57.102904.190139.

54. Rice, J.M. (1913). *Scientific Management in Education*. New York, NY: Publishers Printing Company (p. 3).

55. Pan, S.C., Rickard, T.C. & Bjork, R.A. (2021). Does spelling still matter – and if so, how should it be taught? Perspectives from contemporary and historical research. *Educational Psychology Review*. DOI: 10.1007/s10648-021-09611-y

56. Thomas, M.S.C. and Ansari, D. (2020). Why is neuroscience relevant to education? In Thomas, M., Mareschal, D. & Dumontheil, I.

(Eds) *Educational Neuroscience: Development across the Life Span (Frontiers of Developmental Science)*. Oxfordshire, UK: Routledge.

57. Hattie, J. (2008). *Visible Learning: A Synthesis of Over 800 Meta-analyses Relating to Achievement*. London, UK: Routledge.

58. Stewart, I. & Cohen J. (2000). *The Collapse of Chaos: Discovering Simplicity in a Complex World*. London, UK: Penguin Books (p. 9).

59. Meyer, A.N.D., Payne, V.L., Meeks, D.W., Rao, R. & Singh, H. (2013). Physicians' diagnostic accuracy, confidence, and resource requests: a vignette study. *JAMA Internal Medicine*, 173(21), 1952–1958. DOI: 10.1001/jamainternmed.2013.10081

60. Plomin, R. & Daniels, D. (1987). Why are children in the same family so different from one another? *Behavioral and Brain Sciences*, 10, 1–60.

61. Malanchini, M., Rimfeld, K. Allegrini, A.G., Ritchie, S.J. & Plomin, R. (2020). Cognitive ability and education: how behavioural genetic research has advanced our knowledge and understanding of their association. *Neuroscience and Biobehavioral Reviews*, 111, 229–245. DOI: 10.1016/j.neubiorev.2020.01.016

62. This is an example of an article that tries to capture the complexity of the sociological, neuroscience, epigenetic and psychological evidence on how socioeconomic gaps in early development emerge: McEwen, C.A. & McEwen, B.S. (2017). Social structure, adversity, toxic stress, and intergenerational poverty: An early childhood model. *Annual Review of Sociology*, 43(1), 445–472.

63. Vu, T., Magis-Weinberg, L., Jansen, B.R.J., van Atteveldt, N., Janssen, T.W.P., Lee, N.C., van der Maas, H.L.J., Raijmakers, M.E.J., Sachisthal, M.S.M. & Meeter, M. (2021). Motivation-achievement cycles in learning: a literature review and research agenda. *Educational Psychology Review*. DOI: 10.1007/s10648-021-09616-7

64. There is a noticeable boost in motivation whenever there is a new start – a new topic, the chance to drop subjects – which suggests that children feel released from the baggage of past failures (for a short while at least, until they realise that the playing field is still not level).

65. Nuthall, G. (2007). *The Hidden Lives of Learners*. Wellington, NZ: NZCER Press.

66. Quigley, A. (2018). *Closing the Vocabulary Gap*. Oxfordshire, UK: Taylor & Francis.

67. Boxer, A. (2020, 8 October). What knowledge matters? Being realistic about gaps and recovery [Blog post]. https://achemicalorthodoxy.wordpress.com/2020/10/08/what-knowledge-matters-being-realistic-about-gaps-and-recovery/

68. Sarason, S.B. (1996). *Revisiting 'The Culture of the School and the Problem of Change'*. New York, NY: Teachers College Press (p. 133).

69. Miliband, D. (2004, 8 January). *Personalised Learning: Building A New Relationship with Schools*. Speech to the North of England Education Conference, Belfast, Northern Ireland.

70. The original *Shift Happens* video has been uploaded to YouTube here:
WingedAngel9 (2008, 12 September). *Shift Happens Original* [Video]. YouTube. https://www.youtube.com/watch?v=FdTOFkhaplo

71. Leadbeater, C. (2004). *Learning about Personalisation: How Can We Put the Learner at the Heart of the Education System?* Department for Education and Skills (with the think tank Demos and the National College for School Leadership) Report. Retrieved from https://www.demos.co.uk/files/learningaboutpersonalisation.pdf

72. Ball, S.J. (2008). New philanthropy, new networks and new governance in education. *Political Studies, 56*(4), 747–765.

73. Mansfield, E.D. (1863). The military academy at West Point. *Am. J. Educ.*, 13, 31–33.

74. For an overview of the democratic changes that drive mass education see Dockterman, D. (2018). Insights from 200+ years of personalized learning. *npj Science of Learning*, 3(15), 1–6. DOI: 10.1038/s41539-018-0033-x

75. Barnard, H. (1839). *First Annual Report to the School Commissioners of Connecticut*, as quoted in Monroe, P. ed. (1911). *A Cyclopedia of Education*. New York, NY: The Macmillan Company.

76. Hager, P.E. (1959). Nineteenth century experiments with monitorial teaching. *The Phi Delta Kappan*, 40(4), 164–167. Retrieved from https://www.jstor.org/stable/20342207

77. Lancaster, J. (1821) *The Lancastrian System of Education,* Baltimore, MD: WM. Ogden Niles, p. 31.

78. This blog post lists the generation of words that have been used to describe educational misfits:
Cuban, L. (2020, 6 November). Labeling students then and now (part 1) [Blog post]. https://larrycuban.wordpress.com/2020/11/06/labeling-students-then-and-now-part-1/.

79. Cubberley, E.P. (1916). *Public School Administration: A Statement of the Fundamental Principles Underlying the Organization and Administration of Public Education.* Boston, MA: Houghton Mifflin Company.

80. Sarason, S.B. (1996). *Revisiting 'The Culture of the School and the Problem of Change'.* New York, NY: Teachers College Press (p. 189).

81. Graham, L.J., de Bruin, K., Lassig, C., & Spandagou, I. (2021). State-of-the-art review: a scoping review of 20 years of research on differentiation: investigating conceptualisation, characteristics, and methods used. *Review of Education,* 9(1), 161–198.

82. Willingham, D. & Daniel, D. (2012). Teaching to what students have in common. *Educational Leadership,* 69(5), 16–21. Retrieved from http://www.ascd.org/publications/educational-leadership/feb12/vol69/num05/Teaching-to-What-Students-Have-in-Common.aspx

83. Petrilli, M.J. (2010). All together now? Educating high and low achievers in the same classroom. *Education Next,* 11(1). Retrieved from https://www.educationnext.org/all-together-now/

84. Graham, L.J. & Cologon, K. (2016, 8 March). Explainer: what is differentiation and why is it poorly understood? [Blog post]. https://theconversation.com/explainer-what-is-differentiation-and-why-is-it-poorly-understood-55757

85. McCourt, M. (2019). *Teaching for Mastery.* Woodbridge, UK: John Catt Educational Ltd.

86. Sarason, S.B. (1996). *Revisiting 'The Culture of the School and the Problem of Change'.* New York, NY and London, UK: Teachers College Press.

87. Department for Education and Skills (2006). *2020 Vision: Report of the Teaching and Learning in 2020 Review Group.* Nottingham, UK: DfES. Retrieved from http://www.educationengland.org.uk/documents/pdfs/2006-2020-vision.pdf

88. Bernstein, B. (2000). *Pedagogy, Symbolic Control and Identity: Theory, Research, Critique* (revised). Lanham, MD: Rowman & Littlefield (p. 32).

89. Department for Education and Skills (2006). *2020 Vision: Report of the Teaching and Learning in 2020 Review Group.* Nottingham, UK: DfES. Retrieved from http://www.educationengland.org.uk/documents/pdfs/2006-2020-vision.pdf

90. Maguire, M., Ball, S.J. & Braun, A. (2013). What ever happened to ...? 'Personalised learning' as a case of policy dissipation. *Journal of Education Policy*, 28(3), 322–338 (p. 324). DOI: 10.1080/02680939.2012.724714

91. Maguire, M., Ball, S.J. & Braun, A. (2013). What ever happened to ...? 'Personalised learning' as a case of policy dissipation. *Journal of Education Policy*, 28(3), 322–338. DOI: 10.1080/02680939.2012.724714

92. Kundera, M. (1970). *Laughable Loves.* New York, NY: Faber & Faber (p. 5).

93. In fact, there is evidence to suggest that schools are a relatively minor factor in determining the exam results that students achieve, perhaps accounting for no more than 15% of the differences between outcomes of different schools. See, for example: Wilkinson, D, Bryson, A. & Stokes, L. (2018). Assessing the variance in pupil attainment: How important is the school attended? *National Institute Economic Review*, 243(1), R4–R16. DOI:10.1177/002795011824300110
An analysis by FFT Education Datalab of 2018 key stage 4 (KS4) outcomes demonstrated that more than 50% of the variance between school outcomes at KS4 could be accounted for by differences between students: most significantly the prior attainment of students at the school. The remaining inter-school differences were due to the varying grades achieved by individual students (20%), the in-school variation between subjects (17%) and lastly the

effect of the school itself, which accounted for only 12%. See: Thomson, D. (2020, 20 January). Are we looking in the wrong place to improve attainment? [Blog post]. https://ffteducationdatalab. org.uk/2020/01/are-we-looking-in-the-wrong-place-to-improve-attainment/.

94. Heath, C. & Heath, D. (2007). *Made to Stick: Why Some Ideas Survive and Others Die.* New York, NY: Random House (p. 18).

95. Ofsted (2015, updated 2016, 2018). *School Inspection Handbook: Handbook for Inspecting Schools in England under Section 5 of the Education Act 2005.* London, UK: Ofsted (p. 58).

96. Ofsted (2015, updated 2016, 2018). *School Inspection Handbook: Handbook for Inspecting Schools in England under Section 5 of the Education Act 2005.* London, UK: Ofsted (p. 59).

97. Sources of isomorphism among school leaders are described in chapter 7 of Allen, R. & Sims, S. (2018). *The Teacher Gap.* Abingdon, UK: Routledge.

98. Allen, R. (2019). *How is Data Used in Schools Today? A 2019 Survey of Current Practice.* FFT Education Datalab. Retrieved from https:// fft.org.uk/how-schools-use-data/

99. Allen, R. (2019). *How is Data Used in Schools Today? A 2019 Survey of Current Practice.* FFT Education Datalab. Retrieved from https:// fft.org.uk/how-schools-use-data/

100. Biesta, G.J.J. (2010). Why 'what works' still won't work: from evidence-based education to value-based education. *Studies in Philosophy and Education, 29,* 491–503.

101. Allen, R. (2018, 23 May). What if we cannot measure progress? [Blog post]. https://rebeccaallen.co.uk/2018/05/23/what-if-we-cannot-measure-pupil-progress/

102. White, B. (2018). *Reducing Teacher Workload.* Ashford Teaching Alliance Research Report. Retrieved from https://assets.publishing. service.gov.uk/government/uploads/system/uploads/attachment_data/file/687195/Ashford_Teaching_Alliance_-_Reducing_teacher_workload.pdf

103. James, W. (1902). *The Varieties of Religious Experience.* London, UK: Longmans, Green and Co.

104. Allen, R. & Teacher Workload Advisory Group (2018). *Making Data Work*. Report of the Teacher Workload Advisory Group. London, UK: Department for Education.
Allen, R. (2015). *Seven Things You Might Not Know about Our Schools*. Education Datalab Report. Retrieved from https://ffteducationdatalab.org.uk/2015/03/seven-things-you-might-not-know-about-our-schools/;
Gibson, S., Oliver, L. & Dennison, M. (2015). *Workload Challenge: Analysis of Teacher Consultation Responses*. Research Report DfE-RR445. London, UK: Department for Education.

105. Spielman, A. (2019, 8 June). *Speech to the National Governance Association on 8th June 2019*. Retrieved from https://www.gov.uk/government/speeches/national-governance-association-speech

106. This story is described in: Blastland, M. (2019). *The Hidden Half: How the World Conceals its Secrets*. London, UK: Atlantic Books.

107. Chapter 3 in Blastland, M. (2019). *The Hidden Half: How the World Conceals its Secrets*. London, UK: Atlantic Books (p. 106).

108. Woolf, V. (1931). *The Waves*. Richmond-on-Thames, UK: Hogarth Press (p. 6).

109. Maslow, A.H. (1961). *Towards a Psychology of Being*. New York, NY: Wiley.

110. Young, M.F.D. (Ed.) (1971). *Knowledge and Control: New Directions in the Sociology of Education*. Oxford, UK: Macmillan.

111. Muller, J. (2006). On the shoulders of giants: verticality of knowledge and the school curriculum. In Moore, R., Arnot, M., Beck, J. & Daniels, H. (Eds.) *Knowledge, Power and Educational Reform*. London, UK: Routledge.

112. Shoemaker, B. (1989). *Integrative Education: A Curriculum for the Twenty-First Century*. Oregon School Study Council 33/2 (p. 5).

113. Wilby, P. (2018, 9 October). The counterculture class warrior who turned to Gove. *The Guardian*. Retrieved from https://www.theguardian.com/education/2018/oct/09/counterculture-class-warrior-turned-to-gove
For a fuller discussion of the evolution of Michael F.D. Young's beliefs, see:
Morgan, J. (2015). Michael Young and the politics of the school curriculum. *British Journal of Educational Studies*, 63(1), 5–22. DOI: 10.1080/00071005.2014.983044

114. Young, M.F.D. (2007). *Bringing Knowledge Back In: From Social Constructivism to Social Realism in the Sociology of Education.* Milton Park: Routledge.

115. Hirsch, E.D. (1988). *Cultural Literacy: What Every American Needs to Know.* New York, NY: Random House;Hirsch, E.D. (2016). *Why Knowledge Matters: Rescuing Our Children from Failed Educational Theories.* Cambridge, MA: Harvard Education Press.

116. There are differences in the arguments that Young and Hirsch made, with Hirsch attending more to inequalities in vocabulary and Young more interested in disciplines and disciplinary boundaries. For a list of differences in perspectives, see:
Fordham, M. [@mfordhamhistory] (2018, 12 October). *A short thread follows that looks to find commonalities in the educational thought or Hirsch and Young. There are important differences (I'll get to these at end), but also striking similarities. This is, I suppose, an attempt at nuance...* [Tweet]. Twitter. https://twitter.com/mfordhamhistory/status/1050833650001039362

117. This chapter makes no arguments for or against the idea of powerful knowledge. Read more on the case for powerful knowledge here:
Young, M. & Muller, J. (2013). On the powers of powerful knowledge. *Review of Education,* 1(3), 229–250. DOI: 10.1002/rev3.3017
A philosophical argument against the idea of powerful knowledge can be found here:
White, J. (2018). The weakness of 'powerful knowledge'. *London Review of Education,* 16(2), 325–335. DOI https://doi.org/10.18546/LRE.16.2.11

118. Keil, F. (2006). Explanation and understanding. *Annual Review of Psychology,* 57(1), 227–254 (p. 240). DOI: 10.1146/annurev.psych.57.102904.190100

119. Keil, F. (2006). Explanation and understanding. *Annual Review of Psychology,* 57(1), 227–254. DOI: 10.1146/annurev.psych.57.102904.190100

120. Fordham, M. (2017, 4 March). The curriculum as progression model [Blog post]. https://clioetcetera.com/2017/03/04/the-curriculum-as-progression-model/

121. Counsell, C. (2018, 27 March). In search of senior curriculum leadership: Introduction – a dangerous absence [Blog post]. https://thedignityofthethingblog.wordpress.com/2018/03/27/in-search-of-senior-curriculum-leadership-introduction-a-dangerous-absence/

122. Ofsted (2020). *Initial Teacher Education Framework: A Report on the Responses to the Consultation* [Report]. Retrieved from https://www.gov.uk/government/consultations/initial-teacher-education-inspection-framework-and-handbook-2020-inspecting-the-quality-of-teacher-education/outcome/initial-teacher-education-framework-a-report-on-the-responses-to-the-consultation

123. Young, Michael F.D. & Lambert, D. (2014). *Knowledge and the Future School: Curriculum and Social Justice*. London, UK: Bloomsbury.

124. Hall, S. (2020, 25 July). Knowledge organisers – a failed revolution [Blog post]. https://shallteach.wordpress.com/2020/07/25/knowledge-organisers-a-failed-revolution/

125. Wiliam, D. (2011). *Embedded Formative Assessment*. London, UK: Solution Tree Press.

126. Schwartz, T.(1976). The cargo cult: A Melanesian type-response to change. In DeVos, G.A. (Ed.) *Responses to Change: Society, Culture, and Personality*. New York, NY: Van Nostrand.

127. Stenhouse, L. (1975). *An Introduction to Curriculum Research and Development*. London, UK: Heinemann.

128. Moore Anderson, C. (2020, 31 July). The scales of curriculum planning: Why sequence isn't king [Blog post]. https://cmooreanderson.wixsite.com/teachingbiology/amp/the-scales-of-curriculum-planning-why-sequence-isn-t-king

129. The empirical centrepiece of E.D. Hirsch's book – a rough French data cross-tabulation – does not appear to stand up to scrutiny. For more details see:
Bokhove, C. (2017, 26 April). Hirsch: the case of France [Blog post]. https://bokhove.net/2017/04/26/the-case-of-france/
Furthermore, Education Endowment Foundation evaluations of curriculum programmes such as The Curriculum Centre's Word and World Reading Programme have not signalled success.
See Huat See, B., Gorard, S. and Siddiqui, N. (2015).

Word and World Reading: Evaluation Report. Education Endowment Foundation. Retrieved from https://educationendowmentfoundation.org.uk/projects-and-evaluation/projects/word-and-world-reading-programme/

130. Burnett, F.H. (1911). *The Secret Garden*. London, UK: Heinemann (p. 111).

131. Nuthall, G. (2007). *The Hidden Lives of Learners*. Wellington, NZ: NZCER Press.

132. Question on zero tolerance answered by 6553 teachers on 19 May 2021; question on exclusions answered by 2857 teachers on 10 June 2018 via Teacher Tapp survey app.

133. Answered by 8703 teachers on 23 July 2020 via Teacher Tapp survey app.

134. Answered by 2857 teachers on 16 June 2018 via Teacher Tapp survey app.

135. Answered by 2162 teachers on 3 May 2018 via Teacher Tapp survey app.

136. Hobbiss, M., Sims, S. & Allen, R. (2021). Habit formation limits growth in teacher effectiveness: A review of converging evidence from neuroscience and social science. *Review of Education*, 9(1), 3–23.

137. Wiliam, D. (2018). *Creating the Schools Our Children Need: Why What We're Doing Now Won't Help Much (And What We Can Do Instead)*. Florida: Learning Sciences International (pp. 473–475).

138. Holland, J.H. (2014). *Complexity: A Very Short Introduction (Very Short Introductions)*. Oxford, UK: Oxford University Press.

139. Answered by 3005 teachers on 27 September 2010 via Teacher Tapp survey app.

140. Answered by 5844 teachers on 27 September 2019 via Teacher Tapp survey app.

141. Simon, H.A. (2013). *Administrative Behavior, 4th Edition: A Study of Decision making Processes in Administrative Organisations*. New York, NY: Free Press (pp. 473–475).

142. Flinders, D.J. (1988). Teacher isolation and the new reform. *Journal of Curriculum and Supervision*, 4(1), 17–29.

143. Sarason, S.B. (1993). *You Are Thinking of Teaching? Opportunities, Problems, Realities*. San Francisco, CA: Jossey-Bass.
144. Answered by 5902 teachers on 13 October 2019 via Teacher Tapp survey app.
145. O'Gorman, H.J. (1986). The discovery of pluralistic ignorance: an ironic lesson. *Journal of the History of the Behavioral Sciences*, 22(4), 333–347.
146. Lipsky, M. (1980). *Street-Level Bureaucracy: Dilemmas of the Individual in Public Service*. New York, NY: Russell Sage Foundation.
147. The slogan of the government teacher recruitment campaign at the time of writing.
148. White, B. (2016). *Performativity, Parrhesia and the Practical World of Classroom Teaching*, master's dissertation, King's College London (p. 38).
149. White, B. (2016). *Performativity, Parrhesia and the Practical World of Classroom Teaching*, master's dissertation, King's College London (p. 38).
150. Kennedy, M. (2015). Parsing the practice of teaching. *Journal of Teacher Education*, 67(1), 6–17.
151. Kennedy, M. (2015). Parsing the practice of teaching. *Journal of Teacher Education*, 67(1), 6–17 (p. 13).
152. Sims, S. (2019, 19 February). Four reasons instructional coaching is currently the best-evidenced form of CPD [Blog post]. https://samsims.education/2019/02/19/247/
153. Kennedy, M. (2015). Parsing the practice of teaching, *Journal of Teacher Education*, 67(1), 6–17 (p. 13).
154. Kraft, M.A., Blazar, D. & Hogan, D. (2018). The effect of teacher coaching on instruction and achievement: a meta-analysis of the causal evidence. *Review of Educational Research*, 88(4), 547–588.
155. Knight, J. (2021, 3 February). Three approaches to coaching [Blog post]. https://www.instructionalcoaching.com/three-approaches-to-coaching/
156. Myer, J.W. & Rowan, B. (1977). Institutionalized organizations: formal structure as myth and ceremony. *American Journal of Sociology*, 83(2), 340–363.

157. Plowman, M. (1932, December). Keyserling's Challenge (p. 212), *The Adelphi (New Series), The Adelphi Forum*, London, UK: The Adelphi.

158. Weick, K., Sutcliffe, K. M. & Obstfeld, D. (2005). Organizing and the process of sensemaking. *Organization Science*, 16(4), 409–421.

159. Isabella, L.A. (1990). Evolving interpretations as change unfolds: how managers construe key organisational events. *Academy of Management Journal*, 33(1), 7–41. DOI: 10.5465/256350

160. Isolating the causal impact of school leadership on attainment is extremely hard to do, but as an example of how arguments are made as to its importance see, for example:
Teach for Australia (2017, 12 May). School leadership: it matters more than you think [Blog post]. https://teachforaustralia.org/school-leadership-matters-think/

161. A description of the demographic characteristics of school leaders can be found in:
Allen, R. & Rawal, S. (2013). The demography of school leadership. In Earley, P. (Ed.) *Exploring the School Leadership Landscape: Changing Demands, Changing Realities*. London, UK: Bloomsbury.

162. Scheerens, J. (Ed.) (2012). *School Leadership Effects Revisited: Review and Meta-Analysis of Empirical Studies*. Dordrecht, Germany: Springer;
Tan, C.Y., Gao, L. & Shi, M. (2020). Second-order meta-analysis synthesizing the evidence on associations between school leadership and different school outcomes. *Educational Management Administration & Leadership*. DOI:10.1177/1741143220935456

163. Robinson, V. (2018). *Reduce Change to Increase Improvement*. Thousand Oaks, CA: Sage Publications.

164. Taleb, N.N. (2013). *Antifragile: Things that Gain from Disorder*. London, UK: Penguin Books.

165. Evans, M. (2020). *The ResearchED Guide to Leadership*. Woodbridge, UK: John Catt Educational (pp. 222–223).

166. Weick, K. (1993). The collapse of sensemaking in organizations: the Mann Gulch disaster. *Administrative Science Quarterly*, 3, 628–652.

167. These are the views of Simone Weil, as explained in:
Iacovetti, C. (2018, 17 March). Simone Weil, Reflections on the right use of school studies with a view to the love of God (1942) [Blog

post]. https://medium.com/@chrisiacovetti/simone-weil-reflections-on-the-right-use-of-school-studies-with-a-view-to-the-love-of-god-1942-27a2a9b839f7

168. Newmark, B. (2019). *Why Teach?* Woodbridge, UK: John Catt Educational (p. 38).

169. Sarason, S.B. (1996). *Revisiting 'The Culture of the School and the Problem of Change'*. New York, NY: Teachers College Press (p. 111).

170. Woods, D. et al. (2010) *Behind Human Error*. Farnham: Ashgate (p. 30).

171. Taleb, N.N. (2013). *Antifragile: Things that Gain from Disorder*. London, UK: Penguin Books.

172. Milne, A.A. (1926). *Winnie-the-Pooh* (First edition). London, UK: Methuen and Co. Ltd (p. 10).

173. Harford, T. (2016). *Messy*. London, UK: Little, Brown Book Group.

174. This entire argument is available in:
Allen, R. (2019, 22 September). Nobody knows which schools are good [Blog post]. https://rebeccaallen.co.uk/2019/09/22/nobody-knows-which-schools-are-good/

175. It has been shown in other industries that leaders often have little accurate insight into the reasons for their success. See, for example: Mauboussin, M. (2012). *The Success Equation: Untangling Skill and Luck in Business, Sports, and Investing*, Cambridge, MA: Harvard Business Review Press.

176. Taleb, N.N. (2013). *Antifragile: Things that Gain from Disorder*. London, UK: Penguin Books.

177. Barton, C. (2019). *The ResearchED Guide to Education Myths*. Woodbridge, UK: John Catt.

178. Claxton, G. (2021). *The Future of Teaching: And the Myths That Hold It Back*. Abingdon, UK: Routledge.

179. Spielman, A. (2019, 8 June). Speech to the National Governance Association. Retrieved from https://www.gov.uk/government/speeches/national-governance-association-speech

180. Keil, F. (2006). Explanation and understanding. *Annual Review of Psychology*, 57(1), 227–254 (p. 240). DOI: 10.1146/annurev.psych.57.102904.190100

181. Keil, F. (2006). Explanation and understanding. *Annual Review of Psychology*, 57(1), 227–254 (p. 241). DOI: 10.1146/annurev. psych.57.102904.190100

182. The well-known language in *For Want of a Nail* is attributed to Benjamin Franklin, though the proverb is said to originate from England in the 13th century.

183. Cartwright, N. & Hardie, J. (2012). *Evidence Based Policy: A Practical Guide to Doing it Better*. Oxford, UK: Oxford University Press.

184. Beck, T.E. & Plowman, D.A. (2009). Experiencing rare and unusual events richly: the role of middle managers in animating and guiding organizational interpretation. *Organization Science*, 20, 909–924 (p. 915).

185. Maslow, A.H. (1961). *Towards a Psychology of Being*. New York, NY: Wiley.

186. Arrow, K.J. (2004). Is bounded rationality unboundedly rational? Some ruminations. In Augier, M. & March, J.G. (Eds.) *Models of a Man: Essays in Memory of Herbert A. Simon* (pp. 47–55). Cambridge, MA: MIT Press.

187. Kermode, F. (1967). *The Sense of an Ending: Studies in the Theory of Fiction*. Oxford, UK: Oxford University Press (p. 17).

188. Sutcliffe, K.M. & Obstfeld, D. (2005). Organizing and the process of sensemaking. *Organization Science*, 16(4), 409–421.

189. Young, T. (2014, 8 February). My battle with Michael Gove's blob. *The Spectator*. Retrieved from https://www.spectator.co.uk/article/my-battle-with-michael-gove-s-blob

190. Nicky Morgan, in a speech to the annual conference of the Association of School and College Leaders (ASCL), reported in: Cassidy, S. (2015, 22 March). Minister admits poor children face 'soft bigotry of low expectations' in schools. *The Independent*. Retrieved from https://www.independent.co.uk/news/education/education-news/minister-admits-poor-children-face-soft-bigotry-low-expectations-schools-10125306.html

191. Within classical tragedies, these were classified by Aristotle as Hamartia, which is roughly translated as 'missing the mark' or 'miscalculation'. The contrast between modern and classical tragedies can be found in:

Kierkegaard, S. (1843). *Either/Or, Part I*. Princeton, NJ: Princeton University Press.

192. Eliot, T.S. (1943). *Four Quartets*. San Diego, CA: Harcourt, Brace & Co. (p. 4).

193. This point is made, along with numerous examples, in: Lumby, J. & English, F.W. (2010). *Leadership as Lunacy*. Thousand Oaks, CA: Corwin Publishing.

194. Lovelock, J.E. (1979). *Gaia: A New Look at Life on Earth*. Oxford, UK: Oxford University Press.

195. Watson, A.J. & Lovelock, J.E. (1983). Biological homeostasis of the global environment: the parable of Daisyworld. *Tellus B.*, 35(4), 286–289. DOI:10.1111/j.1600-0889.1983.tb00031.x

196. The main findings outlined can be found in: Tetlock, P.E. (2006). *Expert Political Judgement*. Princeton, NJ: Princeton University Press.

197. Silver, N. (2012). *The Signal and the Noise*. London, UK: Penguin Random House (pp. 53–56 at p. 53 and p. 56).

198. Zellner, A., Keuzenkamp, H.A. & McAleer, M. (Eds) (2002). *Simplicity, Inference and Modelling: Keeping it Sophisticatedly Simple*. Cambridge, UK: Cambridge University Press.

199. Stanton, S. (2021). A Sisyphean endeavour: school complexity and the problem of remote learning [Blog post]. https://thedustytsundoku.wordpress.com/2021/02/22/a-sisyphean-endeavour-school-complexity-and-the-problem-of-remote-learning/

200. Words taken from Michael Gove, referencing Mathew Arnold, in: Gove, M. (2014, 10 July). *Michael Gove Speaks about the Future of Education Reform* [Speech]. Speech to the first Education Reform Summit in London, published by the Department for Education. Retrieved from https://www.gov.uk/government/speeches/michael-gove-speaks-about-the-future-of-education-reform.

201. Lewis, M. (2016). *The Undoing Project: A Friendship That Changed Our Minds*. New York City, NY: W.W. Norton & Co.

202. Gall, J. (1975). *General Systemantics: An Essay on How Systems Work, and Especially How They Fail, Together with the Very First Annotated Compendium of Basic Systems Axioms: A Handbook and Ready*

Reference for Scientists, Engineers, Laboratory Workers, Administrators, Public Officials, Systems Analysts, etc., etc., etc., and the General Public. Ann Arbor, MI: General Systemantics Press (p. 65).

203. Nickow, A., Oreopoulos, P. & Quan, V. (2020). *The Impressive Effects of Tutoring on Pre K-12 Learning: A Systematic Review and Meta-analysis of the Experimental Evidence.* NBER Working Paper 27476. DOI: 10.3386/w27476

204. Note that much pre-2006 policy work was in relation to phonics in general, rather than synthetic phonics. For a short history, see: Chew, J. (2018, 30 July). Phonics developments in England from 1998 to 2018 [Blog post]. https://rrf.org.uk/2018/07/30/phonics-developments-in-england-from-1998-to-2018-by-jenny-chew/

205. Rose, J. (2006). *Independent Review of the Teaching of Early Reading.* Department of Education and Skills, UK.

206. Machin, S., McNally, S. & Viarengo, M. (2018). Changing how literacy is taught: evidence on synthetic phonics. *American Economic Journal: Economic Policy*, 10(2), 217–241.

207. Department for Education (2011). Funding for phonics teaching to improve children's reading [Press release]. Retrieved from https://www.gov.uk/government/news/funding-for-phonics-teaching-to-improve-childrens-reading

208. Department for Education (2012). Phonics screening check and key stage 1 assessments: England 2012 [National Statistics]. Retrieved from https://www.gov.uk/government/statistics/phonics-screening-check-and-national-curriculum-assessments-at-key-stage-1-in-england-2012

209. Department for Education (2021). Validation of systematic synthetic phonics programmes: supporting documentation, Government Guidance. Retrieved from https://www.gov.uk/government/publications/phonics-teaching-materials-core-criteria-and-self-assessment/validation-of-systematic-synthetic-phonics-programmes-supporting-documentation

210. Taleb, N.N. (2013). *Antifragile: Things that Gain from Disorder.* London, UK: Penguin Books Ltd.

211. Silver, N. (2012). *The Signal and the Noise.* London, UK: Penguin Random House.

212. Harari, Y.M. (2018). *21 Lessons for the 21st Century*. London, UK: Jonathan Cape (p. 214).

213. The exact wording of this quote is disputed, as is the original source. For a discussion, see:
Wikiquote (2021). *Talk: Oliver Wendell Holmes Jr*. Wikiquote website. https://en.wikiquote.org/wiki/Talk:Oliver_Wendell_Holmes_Jr

214. Maslow, A.H. (1961). *Towards a Psychology of Being*. New York, NY: Wiley.